Sacred Seasons

A Daily Devotional for Life's Transformations

Dr. Jovan T. Davis

Copyright © 2024 Dr. Jovan T. Davis

All rights reserved

The characters and events portrayed in this book are fictitious. Any similarity to real persons, living or dead, is coincidental and not intended by the author.

No part of this book may be reproduced, or stored in a retrieval system, or transmitted in any form or by any means, electronic, mechanical, photocopying, recording, or otherwise, without express written permission of the publisher.

ISBN-13: 9798882679469

Cover design by: Art Painter
Library of Congress Control Number: 2018675309
Printed in the United States of America

This book is dedicated to all the cherished individuals who have shown me unwavering love throughout all my seasons of life. I am especially grateful for the greatest gifts that God has blessed me with - my beloved children; Jordyn, Trinity, Jayden, and Joshua. Their tender hearts and precious souls have brought light and joy into my life, making each day more meaningful and beautiful than the last.

Contents

Title Page

Copyright

Dedication

Introduction

Preface

Day 1 - The Road Ahead	1
Day 2 - Overcoming the Grasshopper Complex	4
Day 3 - Forgiveness is Freedom	8
Day 4 - Mastering the Mind: A Journey to Renewal	11
Day 5 - Guarding Your Sanctuary: Protect Your Space	14
Day 6 - Navigating the Precious Currency of Trust	17
Day 7 - Mastering Impulses: Walking in Kingdom Authority	20
Day 8 - Transforming Restrictions into Acquistions: Trusting in God's Power	23
Day 9 - Finding Peace in Restlessness	26
Day 10 - Equipping Yourself for the Journey	29
Day 11 - Snip Snip: Cutting Toxic Ties	32
Day 12 - Covered: Living Under Grace	35
Day 13 - Mastering Self-Control for a Blessed Life	38
Day 14 - Awakening to Your True Potential	41

Day 15 - Persevere and Pursue	44
Day 16 - Stay Woke and Vigilant	47
Day 17 - Guarding Your Mental Landscape	49
Day 18 - The Internal Battle: Cultivating the Mind	52
Day 19 - Beware of Diverging Distractions	55
Day 20 - A Call to Authenticity	58
Day 21 - Reach for New Levels of Greatness	61
Day 22 - Overcomer of Adversity	64
Day 23 - Rescued from Despair: The Divine Release	67
Day 24 - The Blueprint of Creation: Where Mind Meets Manifestation	70
Day 25 - Authentic Rejoicing: Genuine Joy Amidst Life's Challenges	73
Day 26 - Breaking the Chains of Routine: Embracing the Wonder of God's Creation	76
Day 27 - Rising Beyond Defeats: The Resilience of Christ's Victory	79
Day 28 - Past Problems, Present Praise	82
Day 29 - Embracing the Giver to Receive the Gift	85
Day 30 - The Power of Resilient Growth	88
Epilogue	91
Acknowledgement	93

Introduction

Embracing the Sacred Seasons

Welcome to "Sacred Seasons: A Daily Devotional for Life's Transformations." Life is a journey marked by a series of seasons—each with its unique blend of joys, challenges, and opportunities for growth. Just as nature experiences the ebb and flow of seasons, so do our lives.

In this devotional, we embark on a 30-day journey, exploring the spiritual significance of the seasons we encounter. Whether you find yourself in the budding hope of spring, the abundant warmth of summer, the tranquil reflections of autumn, or the stillness and contemplation of winter, each day's reflection is designed to resonate with the rhythm of your life.

Discovering the Divine in Every Season: God's handiwork is woven into the fabric of each season, both in the natural world and the seasons of our lives. As we delve into the Scriptures, reflecting on verses that speak to the essence of each season, we'll uncover profound truths that offer guidance, comfort, and inspiration.

Transforming Challenges into Opportunities: Life's transformations can often be challenging, yet they present unique opportunities for spiritual and personal growth. Each day's devotional is crafted to encourage you to see these transformations as sacred moments, inviting you to draw closer to God and experience His transformative power.

Daily Reflections and Practical Applications: Each day includes a Scripture verse, a devotional thought, and practical applications to help you apply the spiritual insights to your daily life. Whether you're navigating a season of change, seeking wisdom, or simply desiring a deeper connection with God, these reflections aim to meet you where you are.

A Journey of Renewal: The goal of this devotional is not only to guide you through the various seasons of life but also to cultivate a sense of renewal and spiritual awakening. By the end of these 30 days, my hope is that you'll emerge with a renewed perspective on life, a strengthened faith, and a deeper awareness of God's presence in every season.

Preface

Embracing the Journey

Welcome to "Sacred Seasons: A Daily Devotional for Life's Transformations." As we embark on this transformative journey together, I am filled with gratitude and anticipation for the moments we will share over the next 30 days.

Life is an intricate tapestry, woven with threads of joy, sorrow, triumphs, and trials. Throughout my years as a motivational speaker, entrepreneur, and educator, I've had the privilege of walking alongside countless individuals navigating the diverse landscapes of their own journeys. It is from these shared experiences and the wellspring of God's wisdom that "Sacred Seasons" was born.

This devotional is more than a collection of reflections; it is a companion for your daily pilgrimage. Each entry is crafted to resonate with the ebb and flow of life's seasons, offering scriptural guidance, heartfelt reflections, and practical insights to illuminate your path. Whether you find yourself in the radiant bloom of spring, the warmth of summer, the contemplative hues of autumn, or the hushed stillness of winter, "Sacred Seasons" is designed to meet you where you are.

The daily readings are not prescriptive but an invitation to pause, reflect, and connect with the divine wisdom that transcends our temporal understanding. My hope is that these pages become a sanctuary—a space where you can find solace, encouragement, and inspiration to face each day with renewed strength.

As we journey together through these sacred seasons, may you discover the transformative power of faith, hope, and love. May the words penned on these pages be a source of comfort and guidance, reminding you that you are not alone on this pilgrimage of life.

May this devotional be a treasured guide on your journey, providing moments of contemplation and enlightenment every day. Embrace the path ahead, and cherish each stage of the sacred seasons.

Warm regards,

Dr. Jovan T. Davis

Day 1 – The Road Ahead

*"Celebrate because your past is always tense,
but your future is perfect."*

Scripture
Jeremiah 29:11 - *"For I know the plans I have for you,"* declares the LORD, *"plans to prosper you and not to harm you, plans to give you hope and a future."*

Facing the Storms of Life:
Have you ever realized how challenging it is to have hope when there is no solution in sight? Have faith when fear is all-consuming? Life's journey can sometimes feel like navigating rough seas with no clear solution in sight. When the rough waves of trials seem to swallow us whole, it gets harder and harder to breathe and to believe that the winds of much-needed change are near. When we find ourselves surrounded by the dark clouds of life, any sense of hope is diminished and it becomes almost impossible to see the light at the end of the tunnel. Yet, the Lord is our anchor, and when we stand steadfast in what He whispers into our spirit, all we need to do is believe.

Belief as Your Rudder:
Belief is like the rudder of a boat. It serves to steer us in the direction of hope even when the manifestation of what is hoped for seems hopeless. It guides us through the dark alleys of defeat and lands us on the shores of victory. It is the thermostat that captures the temperature of our journey, encouraging us to keep on going regardless of the noted reading.

Choosing to Believe:
In this life, we must choose to believe in the promise found in Jeremiah 29:11. It is in this letter to the Babylonian exiles, that Jeremiah reminds them that despite their current situation, God has them on His mind. That despite how things look and feel, God distinctively knows what He has in store for them. And this is the good news; it comes wrapped in prosperity, hope and a future. All they are challenged to do is believe.

Moving Forward in Faith:
God already has extraordinary plans for you and your future. You can celebrate this by knowing that although your past and present may be tense, your future will be perfect. All you need to do is believe and walk obediently aligned to God's will for your life, following every door that He opens. You must continue to move forward without resorting to old habits and self-destructive behavioral patterns. You must focus on the new things that God is doing in your life. Focus on pressing forward as stated in Philippians 3:13-14 and declare that you will strive to move toward all that God has for you. Knowing this, that God is doing a new thing in your life. (Isaiah 43:18-19)

Overcoming Obstacles:
Will the obstacles feel insurmountable? Yes, they will. Will you face moments of defeat? Absolutely. It is inevitably so, that you will encounter moments and seasons of failure, but hold on to this truth, nothing is a complete failure in Christ. Instead, failures are opportunities to grow, learn, and turn your pain into passion and purpose. So, will you stand defeated, dwelling on the past, on regrets, and the things you still have yet to accomplish? Or will you take this opportunity to move forth in experiencing what God has prepared for you. It is time to rise up, pursue the road ahead, and go after your God-given desires with boldness and courage. Ready! Set! Let's go!

Prayer
Dear God, as I journey on the road ahead, help me to see Your presence guiding me. May I not be distracted by the obstacles along the way but trust that You are in complete control. Grant me the strength to believe in Your plans, to move forward obediently, and to focus on the new things You are doing in my life. In moments of defeat, help me find opportunities for growth and turn my pain into passion and purpose. I celebrate the perfect future You have for me. Amen.

∞∞∞

Reflection Question
Facing the Storms of Life:
Share a personal experience where you felt surrounded by challenges, and hope seemed elusive. How did you navigate through that situation?
Belief as Your Rudder:
Reflect on a time when your belief in God's promises served as a guiding force in steering you through difficult circumstances.
Choosing to Believe:
How can you actively choose to believe in God's extraordinary plans for your future, especially when faced with uncertainty or adversity?
Moving Forward in Faith:
What steps can you take to align your life with God's will and focus on the new things He is doing? How can you resist reverting to old habits and patterns?
Overcoming Obstacles:
Think about a specific obstacle or failure you've encountered. How can you turn that experience into an opportunity for growth, learning, and pursuing your God-given desires?
Ready! Set! Let's go!
What bold and courageous steps can you take to pursue the road ahead in alignment with God's plans for your life?
Celebrating the Future:
In what ways can you celebrate the perfect future God has for you, even in the midst of present challenges?

Day 2 - Overcoming the Grasshopper Complex

"A grasshopper's complex reveals not how you see others, but how you genuinely see yourself."

Scripture
Numbers 13:33- *"We saw the Nephilim there (the descendants of Anak come from the Nephilim). We seemed like grasshoppers in our own eyes, and we looked the same to them."*

The Trap of Inferiority:
Have you ever wondered why you could never get to the place of allowing yourself to be joyful over another person's successes and triumphs? Have you ever felt as though someone else's achievements make you feel less than or lacking? This has a name, and it is called the *inferiority complex.* You may feel inferior compared to others. You may find yourself dealing with envy and jealousy because of another's successes. You may even feel unqualified when you look around and measure your abilities against others. But lets make this abundantly clear, in God's eyes you are more than qualified. You are *fearfully and wonderfully made.* (Psalms 139:14). While on the Master Potterer's potter wheel, you were fashioned, formed and fitted with everything you need to be the best you. So stop selling yourself short, your market value is ever-increasing.

Inferiority's Grip:
When you allow inferiority to rule you and when you allow it

to govern your actions. You unknowingly permit it to reveal, not how you see others, but how you genuinely see yourself. Do not allow another person's life to dampen your perspective of yourself, nor let yourself judge others based on your skewed internal condition. Don't be like the Israelite' spies and make, mold or manufacture unnecessary limitations on yourself. When they were charged with the responsibility conferred upon them by Moses to scope out the land God promised them, they allowed the grip of inferiority to strangle their hopes of experiencing the land flowing with milk and honey. They opened the door to sanctioning inferiority with the opportunity to invite doubt into their midst. This doubt caused them to operate through the lens of looking towards self, rather than the faith to look towards God.

Faith Over Doubt:
In times of difficulty, remember that God's 'yes' is still 'yes,' even when self-doubt tries to say 'no.' Doubt contradicts God's words, while faith positions you to collaborate with them. Focus on your progress without falling into the comparison trap; you are capable and qualified because of the One who made you.

Overcoming the Complex:
What must you do? Focus on yourself and your progress without falling into the comparison trap. When you focus on others and their life, you will experience a taste of discontent and dissatisfaction, which is why they are producing, and you are reducing. Do not minimize your abilities and skills. You are capable and qualified at what you do because of Who made you.

What must you do? Take hold of God's word. Allow His word to be *"a lamp unto your feet and a light unto your path."* (Psalms 119:105) Focus on your growth and spiritual development. Seek God as you walk toward purpose. Do not measure yourself according to the standards of the world and those that abide in it. Instead, garner a mindset that declares I am a prototype, not a copycat;

an innovator, not a duplicator; a first-rate version of myself and not a second-rate version of someone else. Take the liberty to measure yourself against the word of God and become whom God has destined you to be. Be you and embrace your true authenticity. Cultivate the best version of yourself and focus on uncovering the beauty locked within your soul.

It is when you allow yourself to do and walk in these things, that you will begin to see the greatness that God has fashioned, formed and fitted within you.

Prayer
Dear God, I thank You for fearfully and wonderfully creating me. Thank You for every component of my life, making me special in Your eyes. Help me overcome the grasshopper complex that distorts my self-perception. Let Your Word be a lamp unto my feet, guiding me away from comparison and towards the uniqueness and authenticity You designed for me. In Jesus' name, I pray. Amen.

∞∞∞

Reflection Questions
The Trap of Inferiority:
Reflect on a time when you felt inferior or less-than due to someone else's achievements. How did it impact your perspective of yourself?
Inferiority's Grip:
How does allowing inferiority to govern your actions influence your interactions with others? In what ways might it distort your self-perception?
Faith Over Doubt:
Share an experience where you had to choose faith over doubt. How did focusing on God's promises help you overcome self-doubt?
Overcoming the Complex:
In what areas of your life do you find yourself falling into the comparison trap? How can you shift your focus from others to your own progress and growth?
What Must You Do?
Consider practical steps you can take to overcome the grasshopper complex. How can you focus on your growth, spiritual development, and authenticity?

Take Hold of God's Word:
How can you make God's Word a guiding light in your life, especially when faced with comparison and feelings of inadequacy?

Embracing True Authenticity:
Reflect on the idea of being a prototype, not a copycat, and an innovator, not a duplicator. How can you embrace your true authenticity and cultivate the best version of yourself?

Day 3 - Forgiveness is Freedom

"Playing the blame game doesn't stop the bleeding, it only creates another incision"

Scripture
Proverbs 10:12 – *"Hatred stirs up strife, but love covers all offenses."*

The Symphony of Life:
Life can be likened to a symphony, with each moment adding a unique blend of challenges, opportunities, victories, defeats, accomplishments, and struggles. All of these elements shape the complex range of emotions that we must navigate within our minds. However, one emotion stands out as particularly restrictive - anger. The battle with anger often reveals a deeper issue: an inability to forgive. This unwillingness to forgive hinders our ability to love and creates countless barriers associated with anger.

The Chains of Unforgiveness:
Unforgiveness is a suffocating weight, dragging us down with its heavy chains. It holds us captive, binding us to negative emotions such as bitterness, resentment, and hurt. With each passing day, the links grow tighter, locking us in our own bodies. It's a soul-stripping emotion that cripples joy and love, leaving us paralyzed in its grasp.

Choosing to Love and Forgive:
What do you do to free yourself from a debilitating and soul-stripping emotion such as anger? The key to freedom is

forgiveness, but most importantly, *love.* Love is a choice, and when we choose to love, we are also choosing to forgive. We cannot forgive without having love in our heart, and we cannot love if we hold onto negative emotions such as hatred, bitterness, jealousy, and envy. We must choose to release ourselves from these emotions, by making the choice to forgive.

Releasing Yourself through Forgiveness:
Pointing fingers and placing blame only perpetuates the cycle of pain. The blame game doesn't heal wounds; it creates new ones that are even harder to mend. On the other hand, forgiveness is like a "get out of jail free" card for you. It's not just for the person who wronged you; it's for your own well-being. By letting go of the harm inflicted upon you by someone else, you are freeing yourself from an internal burden. Forgiveness not only releases the other person, but also liberates you from being a captive of bitterness and resentment.

Choose Freedom:
Can you bear to keep living with the searing pain of fresh wounds, constantly reopened by the blame and resentment? Or will you have the courage to embrace forgiveness and walk towards God's love? The endless cycle of finger-pointing only extends the agony. It is time to break free from this self-inflicted prison. Forgiveness is the key that unlocks the door to freedom, but ultimately it is your choice. Will you take that first step towards healing? The choice rests in your hands, as does the power to set yourself free from the shackles of hurt and anger.

Prayer
Heavenly Father, teach me the art of forgiveness. Help me release the anger and negative emotions that hold me captive. Free me from the chains of unforgiveness and lead me towards complete healing. May I choose love over hatred and find true freedom in Your grace. In Jesus' name, I pray. Amen.

∞∞∞

Reflection Questions
Symphony of Life:
Reflect on a recent moment where anger or resentment played a significant role in your emotions. How did it impact your overall well-being?

Chains of Unforgiveness:
Consider any ongoing conflicts or grudges in your life. How have these emotions acted as heavy chains, restricting your ability to experience joy and love?

Choosing to Love and Forgive:
What does choosing love and forgiveness mean to you? How can you actively make the choice to love and forgive in a specific situation?

Releasing Yourself through Forgiveness:
Reflect on a time when you held onto anger or blame. How did forgiveness release you from that emotional burden?

The Blame Game:
Explore instances in your life where playing the blame game prolonged suffering. How can you break free from this pattern and choose forgiveness instead?

Choose Freedom:
Consider the pain of holding onto grudges. Are you ready to choose freedom through forgiveness? What steps can you take to let go of negative emotions?

The Art of Forgiveness:
How can you actively practice the art of forgiveness in your daily life? Are there specific relationships or situations where forgiveness is needed?

Day 4 - Mastering the Mind: A Journey to Renewal

"You cannot be a mastermind, until you learn how to master your mind"

Scripture

Romans 12:2 - *"Do not be conformed to this world, but be transformed by the renewal of your mind, that by testing you may discern what the will of God is, what is good and acceptable and perfect."*

The Landscape of Our Minds:

In the chaos and noise of everyday life, where do we truly dwell? It is not within our workplaces or with our families, but within the vast landscape of our minds. Our thoughts are constant companions, shaping our actions, influencing our choices, and guiding us through life's journey. The question that arises is: What kind of home have we created within our minds?

Jeremiah's Lament:

In a somber chapter within Lamentations 3, Jeremiah pours out his heart in anguish and sorrow amidst affliction and darkness. He speaks of his suffering as if it were a heavy weight pressing down on him, and he places the blame for his misery on God. But perhaps it was not the circumstances themselves that caused his ongoing grief, but rather the thoughts he chose to dwell on. For our thoughts hold immense power over us, capable of either blessing or cursing us based on the mental dwelling we choose.

Like a double-edged sword, our minds can bring both joy and pain depending on how we wield them.

Mind Mastery and Renewal:
Life mastery begins with mind mastery. To achieve this, we must commit to daily renewal through prayer and the Word of God. The Bible serves as our filter, guiding our thoughts and decisions. The transformation of our mindset requires intentional consumption of content that nourishes our souls, filtering out negativity and falsehoods.

The Power of Recall:
Jeremiah, in verses 21-24, exemplifies the power of recalling God's faithfulness. Returning to what he knew about God, he shifted from hopelessness to hopefulness. This underscores the importance of infusing our minds with God's truths, allowing His Word to govern our thoughts and decisions.

Choosing Your Mental Company:
In Proverbs 23:7, it is stated that our thoughts have the power to shape our reality. To truly be in control of our minds, we must be mindful of the discussions we engage in and the people we surround ourselves with. It is crucial to choose companions who uplift us and drive us towards fulfilling our God-given purpose.

From Slave to Mastermind:
To break free from being a slave to our minds and become the master, we must consciously change our thoughts, filter out negative influences, and carefully select our relationships. By doing so, we gain the ability to overcome obstacles, develop self-control and ultimately shape our own destinies.

Prayer
Lord, help me purge every negative and untrue thought about myself. Grant me the wisdom to bring to mind everything Your Word declares

about me, empowering me to be victorious in my thinking. Surround me with individuals who propel, inspire, and align with Your purpose for my life. Amen.

∞∞∞

Reflection Questions
The Landscape of Your Mind:
Take a moment to reflect on the current state of your mind. How would you describe the landscape of your thoughts? Are there areas that need renewal?
Jeremiah's Lament:
Have you ever experienced a situation where your thoughts intensified your suffering? How can recalling God's faithfulness, as Jeremiah did, transform your perspective in challenging times?
Mind Mastery and Renewal:
How do you currently engage in mind renewal through prayer and the Word of God? Are there specific practices you can implement to intentionally filter out negativity and falsehoods?

The Power of Recall:
Consider a time when recalling God's promises or faithfulness shifted your perspective. How can you cultivate a habit of recalling and meditating on God's truths regularly?
Choosing Your Mental Company:
Evaluate the influences around you. Are the conversations and associations in your life uplifting and aligning with your God-given purpose? What changes can you make to surround yourself with positive influences?
From Slave to Mastermind:
In what areas of your life do you feel like a slave to your thoughts? How can you intentionally change your thoughts, exercise control over your mind, and move towards self-mastery?
Becoming a Mastermind:
Reflect on the quote "You cannot be a mastermind until you learn how to master your mind." What steps can you take today to become the master of your mind?

Day 5 - Guarding Your Sanctuary: Protect Your Space

"You must decide to put people in their proper place rather than in the place they desire to prop"

Scripture
Proverbs 4:23 - *"Above all else, guard your heart, for everything you do flows from it."*

Securing the Valuables:
We pour our time and resources into fortifying our homes, cars, and other prized possessions with state-of-the-art security systems. These elaborate measures are meticulously crafted to ward off potential intruders, and interestingly enough, statistics reveal that the mere presence of a security system is enough to deter 60% of burglars. However, when it comes to safeguarding our personal lives, we may not have physical barriers in place, but we are urged to be just as vigilant in protecting our hearts and emotional well-being within our own space.

People in Their Proper Place:
In our lives, people will gravitate towards the space we allow them to fill. Like burglars seeking out open windows, some individuals will invade our personal boundaries, bringing negativity and emotional weight with them. Proverbs 4:23 warns us to protect our hearts, as all of our actions stem from it.

Identifying Potential Leaches:

Those who prop themselves to us often recognize our potential, even if they don't express it verbally. Their goal is to keep us captive, preventing progress and growth. The saying "misery loves company" holds true. To protect our space, we must distance ourselves from these codependent individuals, creating necessary barriers.

Unhooking the Anchor:
Just like the anchor of a boat holds it back, these individuals seek to keep us from advancing. To unhook their anchor, we must pull the plug on intimate conversations, limit their access to the details of our lives, and cease trusting them with our vulnerabilities.

Prioritizing Your Space:
It's essential to protect your mind, peace, and, above all, your heart. Putting yourself first is not selfish; it's self-preservation. Establishing boundaries, distancing from toxic relationships, and being selective about who shares your space are crucial steps in protecting your sanctuary. Don't be ashame to safeguard your safe haven.

Prayer
Heavenly Father, open my eyes to discern those I should embrace and those I need to release. Guide me on the journey to protect my space, guarding my heart from negative influences. Grant me the wisdom to prioritize my mental and emotional well-being. In Jesus' name, I pray. Amen.

∞∞∞

Reflection Questions

Securing the Valuables:
Reflect on the security measures you have in place for your physical possessions. How intentional are you about safeguarding your personal space, especially your heart?

People in Their Proper Place:
Consider the people in your life. Are there individuals who intrude with criticism, negativity, or emotional burdens? How can you establish boundaries to ensure people are in their proper place?

Identifying Potential Leaches:
Think about the relationships around you. Are there individuals who seem to hinder your progress or growth? How can you identify and distance yourself from potential leaches in your life?

Unhooking the Anchor:
Reflect on the idea of anchors in your life. Are there conversations, details, or vulnerabilities that you should limit sharing with certain individuals? How can you unhook their anchor from holding you back?

Prioritizing Your Space:
Evaluate your priorities. How often do you prioritize your mental and emotional well-being? What steps can you take to establish healthy boundaries and protect your sanctuary?

Deciding People's Place:
Consider the people around you. Are they in the place they desire to be, or have you intentionally placed them where they belong in your life? How can you decide and enforce where people belong in your space?

Day 6 - Navigating the Precious Currency of Trust

"Trust uncensored is trust misappropriated"

Scripture
Psalm 146:3 - *"Do not trust in princes, in mortal man, in whom there is no salvation."*

The Pursuit of Wisdom:
In a world consumed by the pursuit of material possessions and shallow successes, the search for wisdom is often neglected. However, Proverbs 4:7 serves as a powerful reminder that wisdom should be our highest priority and encourages us to seek it tirelessly. But what makes wisdom so essential? Wisdom acts as our guide in discerning who to trust and to what extent, allowing us to navigate the complexities of relationships and decisions with clarity and insight.

Trust: A Precious Currency:
In the game of social interactions, trust is a precious and valuable currency. It is not to be handed out haphazardly, for not everyone or everything is deserving of it. To blindly bestow trust without careful consideration can often lead to disappointment and heartache. Therefore, deciphering whom and what to trust should be a wise and intentional process because trust uncensored is trust misappropriated. Like sifting through grains of sand for diamonds, we must carefully examine each person and situation

before determining if they are worthy of our trust.

Guarding Your Dreams*:*
Not everyone is meant to know the depths of your hopes and dreams. Not everyone is meant to see your vision. There will be moments when you will disclose God-driven intimate revelations to people who will not understand its true depths. Why? Because those revelations were only meant for you to experience. The thing that lead to Joseph's confrontation with his brothers is that he gave sight to a dream that others were only able to see as a nightmare. The idea of him ruling over his brothers was horrendous, therefore any effort devised to prevent it from happening was deemed heroic in their eyes.

Facing Criticism and Mockery:
In the pursuit of your goals, be prepared for criticism and mockery. People may take advantage of you or belittle your dreams. Therefore, trust prudently and censor your conversations wisely. Not everyone needs access to your most intimate revelations, and discernment is key in protecting your dreams from unnecessary opposition.

Connect to the Source of Wisdom:
To acquire wisdom, connect with the One who possesses boundless wisdom. James 1:5 encourages us to ask God for wisdom, and it will be generously given. In prayer, seek the wisdom that honors God in your actions and words. As you navigate life's journey, may God's wisdom guide you in discerning whom to trust and in safeguarding the precious currency of trust.

Prayer
Heavenly Father, gift me with the wisdom that allows me to honor You in all that I do and say. Help me discern whom and what to trust,

guarding my dreams and aspirations. Grant me the discernment to wisely censor my conversations and share only what aligns with Your purpose for my life. In Jesus' name, I pray. Amen.

∞∞∞

Reflection Questions
The Pursuit of Wisdom:
How do you prioritize the pursuit of wisdom in your life amidst the world's focus on material possessions and superficial gains?
Trust: A Precious Currency:
Reflect on the concept of trust as a precious currency. In what areas of your life have you placed trust without thorough consideration? How has blind trust impacted you in the past?
Guarding Your Dreams:
Consider the dreams and aspirations you have. Are there moments when you've faced criticism or mockery for sharing your vision with others? How can you be more discerning in whom you share your most intimate revelations with?

Facing Criticism and Mockery:
Reflect on Joseph's story and how he faced opposition from his brothers due to sharing his dreams. Have you experienced opposition or criticism for your dreams? How did you handle it, and what did you learn from those experiences?
Connect to the Source of Wisdom:
How intentional are you about connecting with God, the ultimate source of wisdom, in prayer? How has seeking God's wisdom influenced your decision-making and discernment in navigating life's journey?
Trust Uncensored:
Consider the phrase "trust uncensored is trust misappropriated." In what situations have you experienced misappropriated trust? How can you become more intentional and discerning in whom and what you trust?

Day 7 – Mastering Impulses: Walking in Kingdom Authority

"Don't act on impulse but on His pulse"

Scripture

Ecclesiastes 5:2 – *"Do not be hasty in word or impulsive in thought to bring up a matter in the presence of God. For God is in heaven, and you are on the earth; therefore, let your words be few."*

The Pitfalls of Impulsivity:
Impulsivity, if left unchecked, can lead to unnecessary struggles and problems. The urge to act without thinking can often result in a downward spiral, causing you to dive into avoidable troubles and conflicts. Not only is impulsivity self-destructive, but it also has the potential to harm those around you, leaving a trail of chaos and hurt in its wake.

The key to overcoming impulsive behaviors is to surrender your thoughts and internal conflicts to God. As you filter them through His Word and seek His will, you will find clarity and guidance amidst the maze of emotions that can often overwhelm us.

Navigating the Maze of Emotions:
The world of emotions is complex and unpredictable, but by taking the time to pray about them and seeking patience in discerning how to respond, we can gain control over our impulses.

This intentional mental process requires practice and time, much like learning any new skill. Developing spiritual habits, such as prayer and seeking guidance from God, is crucial for intentionally walking in faith and navigating the intricate web of our emotions.

Steering Clear of Sinful Paths:
Impulsivity stems from our behaviors, and when we give into it, we surrender to our fleshly desires. These actions are often driven by sin and can lead us away from God's purpose for our lives. To combat impulsivity, we must closely monitor our behaviors and the underlying emotions. This requires a vigilant mind and careful discernment.

Acting on His Pulse:
Living a faith-filled life and embodying the kingdom of God requires governing our emotions. Acting on God's pulse, not our impulsive nature, allows us to pursue godly ways and reflect the image of Jesus Christ. As we walk in kingdom authority, our lives become a testament to the power of God and the eternal nature of His kingdom. Others are watching, and our example can encourage them to do the same.

Prayer
Heavenly Father, teach me Your ways, and direct my steps. May all that I do and say bring glory and honor to You. Help me overcome impulsive behaviors and walk in discernment, acting on Your pulse rather than my fleeting emotions. In Jesus' name, I pray. Amen.

∞ ∞ ∞

Reflection Questions
The Pitfalls of Impulsivity:
Reflect on a time when impulsive behavior led to unnecessary struggles or problems. What lessons did you learn from that experience?

Navigating the Maze of Emotions:
How do you currently navigate and process your emotions? In what ways can prayer and seeking patience help you discern the root causes of your feelings?

Steering Clear of Sinful Paths:
Consider the connection between impulsivity and sinful behavior. Are there specific behaviors or actions that you recognize as impulsive and potentially sinful? How can you be more vigilant over your mind to walk in discernment?

Acting on His Pulse:
Reflect on the idea of acting on God's pulse rather than your impulsive nature. In what areas of your life do you struggle to align your actions with God's will? How can you intentionally embody the kingdom of God in your daily actions?

Day 8 – Transforming Restrictions into Acquisitions: Trusting in God's Power

"God's power can transform restrictions into acquisitions"

Scripture
Luke 1:37 – *"For nothing will be impossible with God."*

Shifting Perspective:
It's effortless to become fixated on our shortcomings instead of cherishing the blessings bestowed upon us. Each new day is a chance to embrace the abundance and grace gifted to us by God, and to cultivate a spirit of thankfulness within our hearts. When faced with adversity and struggles, do we succumb to the world's predictions or place our trust in God's unwavering promises? Let us never forget that what may appear impossible for us, is entirely possible for the all-knowing and all-powerful God who guides us through life's journey.

The Story of Transformation:
In Acts 3, a man who had been crippled since birth sat slumped at the temple gate, his legs twisted and useless beneath him. The weight of his disability weighed heavily on him, and he felt as though he would never escape from its grasp. But then, through the power of God, all things changed. Through the unwavering faith of the disciples and the crippled man himself, God's miraculous hand reached down and transformed his limitations into blessings. What once seemed insurmountable became a powerful testimony to God's ability to bring about change. His life

was forever altered, a living demonstration that with God on our side, even the most impossible situations can be turned around for our good.

Facing Uncertainties with Faith:
While uncertainties about the future exist, one constant assurance is God's power to transform restrictions into acquisitions. Your situation can be turned in your favor. The primary challenge lies in our faith and belief in God's promises. Address the root of disbelief, uncover the reasons hindering trust, and work towards resolving them. Trust serves as the conduit connecting us to God's power.

Dealing with Trust Issues:
Unresolved trust issues from the past can affect our ability to trust God. Disappointment, broken trust, and lies can create deep-rooted issues. To step into freedom, address these trust issues and heal. Remember, humanity may fail, but God is perfect and forever faithful. Trust that He can remove the restrictions on your promised acquisitions.

Prayer
Heavenly Father, even in a world filled with uncertainties, I choose to put my complete trust in You. I exercise steadfast trust, knowing that You can transform my restrictions into acquisitions. You are in control of my life, and I believe in Your transformative power. Amen.

∞∞∞

Reflection Questions
Shifting Perspective:
Reflect on a recent situation where you faced challenges or limitations. How

might shifting your perspective and focusing on God's promises change your outlook on those challenges?

The Story of Transformation:
Consider the story in Acts 3 where God's power transformed a man's life. Are there areas in your life where you need God's transformative power? How can you exercise faith and trust in God's ability to turn challenges into opportunities?

Facing Uncertainties with Faith:
Identify any uncertainties or fears about the future that you may be currently facing. How can you strengthen your faith and trust in God's promises to navigate through these uncertainties?

Dealing with Trust Issues:
Reflect on any past disappointments, broken trust, or lies that may have affected your ability to trust, both in human relationships and in God. How can you address and heal these trust issues to deepen your reliance on God's perfect and faithful nature?

Day 9 – Finding Peace in Restlessness

"Rest is important for a believer because a restless believer can become a reckless believer"

Scripture
Philippians 4:6-7 - *"Be anxious for nothing, but in everything by prayer and supplication with thanksgiving let your requests be made known to God. And the peace of God, which transcends all understanding, will guard your hearts and minds in Christ Jesus."*

The Overwhelming Blur:
Life can often feel like a constant blur of never-ending obligations, obstacles, and concerns. From the demanding pressures of work and parenthood to the constant weight of financial burdens and marital issues, it can be easy to become consumed by these responsibilities. As we navigate through this storm of stress, anxiety and restlessness can cling to us like unwelcome companions, tempting us with temporary solutions and pushing us towards impulsive choices.

Finding Calm in Chaos:
Amidst the chaos of life, turning to Jesus Christ is the best solution. Rather than giving in to impulsive actions and beliefs, let Jesus be your source of peace. Pray to Him, make your requests known, and give thanks for all that He has done. As Paul reminds us, God's peace, which surpasses understanding, can protect our hearts and minds through Christ Jesus. With His power, Jesus can bring calmness to the chaos we face in our lives.

The Problem of Focus:
Often, our struggle lies in misplaced focus. We concentrate on the problems rather than the promises, on hopelessness rather than anchoring our emotions in God. A restless believer tends to become reckless in decisions. It's crucial to redirect our thoughts towards life, hope, and belief. Understand that your focus impacts your emotions, and your emotions guide your actions. Are your decisions fueled by restlessness and anxiety, or are they grounded in peace?

Refocusing on God's Promises:
Learn the art of refocusing. Shift your focus from problems to promises, from hopelessness to trusting in God. Embrace the truth that whatever captures your attention will influence your emotions and, in turn, determine your actions. If restlessness and anxiety prevail, it's time to seek God persistently, pray, and focus on His promises.

Rest is Crucial:
As a believer, true rest goes beyond just physical relaxation but also encompasses a deep sense of peace and contentment found in Christ. A restless believer, consumed by constant worry and turmoil, is at risk of acting recklessly. Instead, turn to God and follow His path to inner peace, drawing upon His unwavering strength and limitless power to navigate through life's inevitable challenges with grace and confidence.

Prayer

Heavenly Father, in moments of restlessness and anxiety, I turn to You. Lead me on the pathway of peace. Help me refocus on Your promises rather than problems. Grant me the wisdom to make decisions grounded in Your peace. Amen.

∞∞∞

Reflection Questions

The Overwhelming Blur:
Reflect on the different responsibilities and challenges in your life that sometimes feel overwhelming. How do you typically respond to these situations? Are there healthy ways you can address the feeling of being overwhelmed?

Finding Calm in Chaos:
Consider a recent time when you felt anxious or restless. How might entrusting your anxieties to Jesus through prayer, supplication, and thanksgiving bring a sense of calm to your situation?

The Problem of Focus:
Evaluate where your focus lies in challenging situations. Are you more focused on the problems or the promises of God? How can you intentionally shift your focus from hopelessness to trusting in God's promises?

Refocusing on God's Promises:
Identify a specific promise from God's Word that you can hold onto in times of restlessness. How can you incorporate that promise into your daily thoughts and actions?

Rest is Crucial:
Consider the importance of rest, not just in a physical sense but as a state of peace in Christ. In what ways can you prioritize and cultivate this rest in your life?

Day 10 - Equipping Yourself for the Journey

"Preparation is the act of seeing yourself already there, even before you get there"

Scripture

Hebrews 11:1 - *"Now faith is confidence in what we hope for and assurance about what we do not see."*

The United Dream:
Despite our varied backgrounds and experiences, we are united by a common thread - the dream that burns within each of us. Some will see their dreams take shape and transform into reality, while others may stumble and fall short due to the overwhelming grip of fear. But one thing remains certain - dreams do not manifest on their own; they demand hard work, unwavering commitment, and unrelenting perseverance. Many may yearn for success, yet attempt to bypass the necessary process of growth and learning.

The Learning Process:
As we embark on our journey to manifest our dreams, the learning process becomes paramount. It is through this process that we mold ourselves, refining our abilities and perfecting our art. Keep in mind that your dream must first exist as a vibrant reality within your mind before it can take shape in the physical world. Preparation requires visualizing yourself already having achieved your goal, long before you actually reach it. See yourself standing proudly at the finish line, basking in the glow of success like a

radiant sun beaming down upon you.

Prepare and Equip Yourself:
Today, take intentional steps to prepare and equip yourself for the journey. Believe that you've already arrived at your desired destination. Cultivate faith, take action, and commit to the hard work required to achieve your goals. Are you committed to your journey? Are you equipping yourself with the knowledge and resources needed? Actively engage in the process of creating and designing the life you envision.

Bold Dreams and Overcoming Fear:
Dream your dream boldly and dare to overcome the paralyzing fear that hinders progress. Have faith, get to work, and refuse to let fear rob you of the glory that comes from achieving your aspirations. The learning process is where you develop the resilience, skills, and mindset needed to turn your dreams into reality.

Prayer

Heavenly Father, I am grateful for Your guidance and direction. Grant me the wisdom to be attentive to every direction You provide. May my dreams and aspirations bring glory to Your name as I actively engage in the process of preparation and equipping. Amen.

∞∞∞

Reflection Questions
The United Dream:
Consider the dream or vision you carry within. How clearly can you articulate this dream? Do you believe in the possibility of its manifestation?

The Learning Process:
Reflect on the learning process in your journey toward your dreams. What

specific skills or knowledge do you feel are crucial for your success? How are you actively engaging in the process of preparation?

Prepare and Equip Yourself:
Explore your commitment level to your journey. Are you actively equipping yourself with the knowledge and resources needed for your dreams? How can you enhance your preparation efforts?

Bold Dreams and Overcoming Fear:
Examine any fears or doubts that may be hindering your progress. How can you overcome these fears and move forward boldly in pursuing your dreams? Are there specific actions you can take to confront and conquer your fears?

Preparation is the Act:
Embrace the idea that preparation involves seeing yourself already at your desired destination. How can you actively visualize and internalize the success of your dreams? What practical steps can you take to embody the reality of your envisioned future?

Day 11 - Snip Snip: Cutting Toxic Ties

"Sometimes you have to take the initiative to tell some people that their lease is up. You can no longer use me or abuse me"

Scripture
1 Corinthians 15:33 - "Do not be deceived: 'Bad company ruins good morals."

Identifying Toxic Relationships:
As we journey through life, we will encounter a myriad of individuals who enter our lives and impact us in various ways. Some will enrich our experiences and bring joy to our days, while others will drain us of energy and leave us feeling depleted. It is crucial that we discern between the two and end any relationships that do not contribute positively to our growth. At times, it falls upon us to take the first step and communicate to certain individuals that their presence in our lives has come to an end. Just as a tenant's lease expires, so too must some relationships come to a close for our own well-being.

Ending Unhealthy Leases:
There are individuals who have long overstayed their welcome in our lives, like stubborn roots digging deep into the soil of our minds and hearts. They take up space without bringing any nourishment or growth. It is crucial to assert that their season of misuse and abuse is over. We must evict them from our inner spaces and make room for a new tenant - one who brings light and

warmth, who guides us towards our true potential and empowers us to reach it. This new resident challenges our old beliefs and behaviors, correcting them with gentle conviction. They offer assistance during tough times and provide hope for a brighter future ahead. Like a lighthouse guiding ships through choppy waters, this new presence within us shines a beacon of positivity and strength, leading us towards a more fulfilling life.

Guarding Your Heart:
According to 1 Corinthians 15:33, "Bad company ruins good morals." This is a reminder that unhealthy relationships can negatively impact your sense of self. It's important to not allow others' opinions and behaviors to dictate how you view yourself. Protect your heart by setting boundaries and using the "EZ Clamps" method to detach from those who are draining your energy. Make it a priority to prioritize your mental, spiritual, physical, and emotional well-being.

Be Picky about Relationships:
Be watchful of whom you listen to and what advice you choose to take into consideration. Not all advice is good advice, nor does it come from a good place. Your surroundings influence you, so choose friendships and relationships that nurture your soul and spirit. So be extra picky and love yourself enough to surround yourself with those who uplift, encourage, and genuinely care.

Prayer
Lord, search my surroundings. Guide me to discern truth and grant me the courage to distance myself from relationships that compromise good morals. Help me release falsehoods and open my eyes to my true value. Walk with me on the journey to cultivate healthy, nurturing connections. Amen.

∞∞∞

Reflection Questions
Identifying Toxic Relationships:
Take a moment to evaluate your relationships. Are there people in your life who consistently drain your energy, add negativity, or hinder your personal growth? How can you identify and differentiate between relationships that add value and those that are toxic?

Ending Unhealthy Leases:
Reflect on any relationships that might have overstayed their welcome in your life. What steps can you take to communicate that their season of misuse and abuse is over? How can you create space for new, empowering relationships?

Guarding Your Heart:
Consider the impact of toxic relationships on your identity and well-being. How can you guard your heart more diligently and use "EZ Clamps" to cut ties with those who drain you? What practices or boundaries can you implement to prioritize your mental, spiritual, physical, and emotional health?

Be Picky about Relationships:
Reflect on the advice and influence you allow into your life. How discerning are you about the relationships you engage in? Are there specific criteria you can establish to be more selective in choosing friendships and relationships that nurture your soul?

Taking Initiative:
Consider situations where you need to take the initiative to end toxic relationships. What steps can you take to communicate boundaries or distance yourself from negativity? How can you prioritize your well-being and assertively convey that certain relationships are no longer serving you?

Day 12 - Covered: Living Under Grace

*"Don't willfully sin because you have grace but
willfully serve because you've been graced!"*

Scripture

Acts 20:28 - *"Be shepherds of the church of God, which he bought with his own blood."*

Grace, Continuous and Ongoing:

The concept of grace is not a mere introduction, but rather a perpetual and ever-flowing gift. As devout followers of Christ, we are enveloped in the protection of His blood, shed on the cross for our salvation. In Romans 5:1-2, we are reassured that through our faith, we are able to fully embrace this unending grace in which we stand. This standing is not an open invitation to recklessly indulge in sin, but rather an empowering force to intentionally serve because we have been blessed with such abundant grace.

Paul's Thorn and God's Response:

Paul fought with a persistent problem, begging God to take it away. But God's answer was unexpected. Rather than removing the problem, He reminded Paul of the grace that surrounds him. It is through our weaknesses that God's power is fully displayed. This teaches us to shift our focus from our weaknesses to the grace that sustains us.

Redemption and Forgiveness:

When you've accepted Jesus as your Savior, you are redeemed and forgiven. Past, present, and future sins are covered by the blood of Christ. This grace doesn't encourage intentional sin but provides assurance that when you fall, grace will lift you; when weak, grace will strengthen you; when troubled, grace will shelter you; when bound, grace will set you free; and when you err, grace will forgive you.

Walking in Grace Daily:
As you go about your days, remember that God's loving gaze is not drawn to your faults or imperfections, but rather to the beautiful grace that surrounds and supports you. Allow yourself to bask in this knowledge and let it ignite a fire of joy and thankfulness within you. Let this grace be the driving force behind each action and service you undertake, guiding you with its warmth and strength. Embrace the power of gratitude and let it fuel your every step as you walk in the light of divine love.

Prayer
Lord, I Thank You For The Unmerited Grace That Covers Me. Help Me To Walk Daily In The Assurance Of Your Forgiveness And Redemption. Empower Me To Serve Joyfully, Knowing That I Stand In Your Grace. Amen.

∞∞∞

Reflection Questions
Understanding Grace:
How would you describe your understanding of grace? Do you see it as a continuous and ongoing gift, or do you sometimes view it as a one-time event? How does Romans 5:1-2 shape your perspective on standing in grace through faith?
Dealing with Weakness:
Reflect on a time when you felt weak or faced challenges. How did you respond to those weaknesses? How can you shift your focus from weaknesses to the empowering grace in which you stand, as illustrated in Paul's experience with the thorn in his flesh?
Redemption and Forgiveness:

Consider the concept of redemption and forgiveness through the blood of Christ. How does this assurance impact your daily life and choices? In what ways can you actively live in the reality of being covered by grace, knowing that past, present, and future sins are forgiven?

Empowerment to Serve:

The devotional suggests that grace should not lead to willful sin but should empower willful service. How does the awareness of God's grace impact your attitude toward serving others? How can you actively let grace empower you to serve joyfully, even in challenging situations?

Facing Scrutiny:

Have you ever felt scrutinized or judged by others, especially in your Christian walk? How can the understanding of God's grace shift your focus away from human scrutiny to the assurance that God sees you through the lens of grace?

Day 13 - Mastering Self-Control for a Blessed Life

"A controlled self is a blessed self"

Scripture
Proverbs 25:28 - "*A man without self-control is like a city broken into and left without walls.*"

The Battle for Self-Control:
The constant battle for self-control wages on, with fiery emotions and impulsive words constantly vying for dominance. At times, it can feel overwhelming, the weight of it all threatening to crush you. But know this: the struggle is not unique to you. It is a universal challenge that we all face. And while it may seem like an insurmountable task, the rewards for conquering it are immeasurable. For within you lies the power of self-control, bestowed upon you by a higher being. Learning to harness this power is essential for your overall well-being, bringing peace and order to a chaotic world.

God's Gift of Self-Control:
Recognize that God has gifted you with the spirit of love, power, and self-control (2 Timothy 1:7). This divine endowment is your source of strength in moments of weakness. God desires to help you overcome the challenges of self-control, ensuring that your actions and words align with His love and wisdom.

The Impact of Unchecked Actions:

When self-control falters, the consequences can be severe. Unchecked emotions and thoughtless words can cause harm to yourself and those around you. Like a city without walls, vulnerabilities emerge, leading to pain and destruction. But there's hope, as God's grace provides a way to overcome these challenges.

Plugging Into God:
Plug yourself into God, the ultimate source of help and guidance. Allow His spirit to work within you, fostering self-control and patience. 2 Timothy 1:7 reminds us that God's spirit is not one of fear but of love, power, and self-control. By aligning with God, you can transform your life and move closer to your desired blessings.

Walking Toward Blessings:
The path to your blessings and true self lies beyond the borders of self-control and patience. As you diligently cultivate these virtues and immerse yourself in your faith, a serene tranquility will settle over your being, bringing with it clarity and inner peace. Step forward on your journey towards blessings, drawing closer to God and embracing His boundless love, unrivaled peace, unbridled joy, eternal salvation, profound healing, and ultimate deliverance. The road may be difficult at times, but the rewards are immeasurable as you continue to grow and evolve on your spiritual path.

Prayer

Lord, grant me the strength to exercise self-control in all areas of my life. Remove anything hindering me from honoring and pleasing you. I desire to align my actions and words with your love and wisdom. Amen.

∞∞∞

Reflection Questions

Understanding Self-Control:
Reflect on times when you struggled with self-control. What were the circumstances, and how did you respond? How do you understand the concept of self-control in light of the biblical perspective presented in the devotional?

God's Gift of Self-Control:
How does knowing that God has equipped you with the spirit of self-control (2 Timothy 1:7) impact your approach to overcoming challenges in this area? What steps can you take to tap into this divine source of strength when faced with moments of weakness?

Consequences of Unchecked Actions:
Think about instances where unchecked emotions or thoughtless words led to negative consequences. How do you relate to the analogy of a city without walls when considering the importance of self-control in safeguarding against vulnerabilities and harm?

Plugging Into God:
In what ways do you currently plug into God for guidance and support in developing self-control? How can you deepen your connection with Him to foster greater self-control and patience in your life?

Walking Toward Blessings:
Reflect on the correlation between self-control and blessings in your life. How do you envision experiencing inner peace, calmness, and mental clarity as you continue to develop self-control and draw nearer to God?

Day 14 - Awakening to Your True Potential

"Your potential is waiting on its recognition"

Scripture

Ephesians 5:14 - *"For this reason it says, 'Awake, sleeper, and arise from the dead, and Christ will shine on you."*

The Power of Awareness:
In a state of heightened awareness, the world around you becomes alive with possibility. It's a moment of crystal-clear clarity, where you gain deep understanding of who you are, where you stand, and what your future holds. This profound awakening sparks a surge of creative energy, unearthing buried ideas and igniting a renewed passion for exploring new ventures. Just as Ephesians 5:14 implores us to awaken from our slumber, in this state we are bathed in the radiant light of Christ, illuminating our innermost thoughts and desires. As if shaking off the cobwebs of complacency, we are fully present and ready to embrace all that life has to offer.

Uncovering Your Potential:
Discovering your potential can take time. Layers of doubt, fear, and low self-esteem may obscure your true identity. Many struggle with limiting beliefs ingrained since childhood. To recognize your potential, you need a reset. Remove the spam of negative programming and pursue inner healing. Reboot your

mental, emotional, and spiritual database with God's ways and your identity in Him.

Daily Affirmations and Positive Influences:
Hit the reset button daily with optimistic affirmations. Surround yourself with positive influencers who encourage and uplift. Your potential waits for recognition, and the journey to self-discovery requires intentional efforts. Remove the years of negative programming, and download God's truth into your renewed mind.

Recognizing Your True Self:
Like a butterfly emerging from its cocoon, recognizing your true self is the key to unlocking your full potential. As you awaken to the person you are in Christ, you gain a clearer understanding of the unique gifts and talents that make you who you are. Shedding the layers of doubt and fear that have held you back, you step into an awakened state where you can fully grasp the magnitude of your potential. The brilliance of your inner light shines brightly, illuminating the path towards your destiny. Embrace this awakening and let it guide you towards all that you were meant to be.

Prayer

Lord, open my eyes to see Your plans for me. Help me remove the layers of doubt and fear that have hindered my potential. Strengthen me to operate according to Your will, recognizing the gifts and talents You've bestowed upon me. Amen.

∞∞∞

Reflection Questions
Power of Awareness:
Share a moment from your life when you experienced a significant awakening

or moment of clarity. How did this awareness impact your understanding of yourself and your future? How does the concept of Christ's light shining upon you resonate with your experiences of awakening?

Uncovering Your Potential:
Reflect on any self-limiting beliefs or doubts that may have hindered your recognition of your true identity and potential. What steps can you take to initiate a reset in your mental, emotional, and spiritual aspects, aligning yourself with God's truth and your identity in Him?

Daily Affirmations and Positive Influences:
Do you currently incorporate daily affirmations into your routine? How do positive influences and encouraging relationships contribute to your journey of self-discovery and potential realization? Share specific affirmations or influences that have had a positive impact on you.

Recognizing Your True Self:
In what ways do you currently recognize and embrace your true self in Christ? Share instances where shedding layers of doubt and fear allowed you to grasp the magnitude of your potential. How has your understanding of your gifts and talents evolved in this process?

Day 15 - Persevere and Pursue

"Good things come to those who chase after them. Stop waiting for it to come to you and you go after it"

Scripture

James 1:4 - *"Let this endurance complete its work so that you may be fully mature, complete, and lacking in nothing."*

Chasing Your Dreams:
The old adage "good things come to those who wait" has been passed down through generations, but its true meaning can be misleading. While patience is certainly a virtue, success requires more than just waiting for it to happen. It demands action, determination, and an unyielding pursuit. Abram, the Father of many nations, did not achieve this title by simply sitting and waiting. He obeyed God's call to move and took bold steps towards his destiny. Ruth, in her quest for love, made courageous decisions that ultimately led her to finding her Boaz. And Nehemiah, tasked with rebuilding Jerusalem, had to leave the comforts of the King's palace and take action to lead the Israelites towards their goal. Waiting may have been part of their journey, but it was action and determination that ultimately brought them success. Just like a river needs steady motion to flow, our dreams require us to take leaps of faith and make moves towards making them a reality.

Embrace Action:
Don't sit idly by, waiting for success to come knocking on your door. Instead, actively pursue your dreams with unwavering determination and relentless effort. Seek guidance from God and

ask for opportunities and strategies to achieve your goals. Equip yourself with knowledge and skills to navigate the journey ahead. Remember, while God may open doors, it's ultimately up to you to take that step forward and make the necessary decisions.

Overcoming Obstacles:
Expect obstacles and failures along the way, but don't let them deter you. Learn from your mistakes, tap into your creativity, and remain innovative and resourceful. Perseverance requires tunnel vision towards your goals, refusing to let anything stand in your way. Build momentum through hard work and unwavering commitment, knowing that each step forward brings you closer to your dreams.

Prayer
Lord, Guide Me On The Path To My Dreams. Help Me Recognize The Opportunities You Place Before Me And Give Me The Courage To Pursue Them With Determination And Faith. Grant Me The Strength To Overcome Obstacles And The Wisdom To Learn From Failures. May I Never Lose Sight Of The Vision You've Placed Within Me. Amen.

∞∞∞

Reflection Questions
Chasing Your Dreams:
What are some dreams or goals that you have been waiting on rather than actively pursuing? How can you incorporate a sense of determined action into your pursuit of these dreams? Share any instances where taking courageous steps led to positive outcomes in your life.
Embrace Action:
Reflect on your current approach to achieving your goals. Are you actively seeking opportunities, equipping yourself with the necessary skills, and making decisions that align with your aspirations? How can you incorporate prayer and reliance on God's guidance into your pursuit of success?
Overcoming Obstacles:
Consider a recent obstacle or failure you encountered in your journey. How did you respond to it, and what did you learn from the experience? Share strategies

or mindset shifts that helped you persevere through challenges. How can you leverage creativity and resourcefulness to overcome future obstacles?

Taking Initiative:

In what areas of your life do you feel the need to take more initiative and actively pursue your goals? How can you build momentum through hard work and commitment? Reflect on the balance between trusting in God's guidance and taking personal responsibility for your actions.

Day 16 – Stay Woke and Vigilant

*"When you are at the table, carefully look at the menu
to ensure that you are not the one being served."*

Scripture

Matthew 24:4-5 - "*And Jesus answered and said to them, 'See to it that no one misleads you. For many will come in My name, saying, I am the Christ, and will mislead many.*"

Stay Woke:
In a world filled with endless distractions and deceptive influences, Jesus warns us to stay woke and not be misled. Like a lighthouse guiding ships through treacherous waters, we must keep our eyes wide open and actively observe the people and situations around us. Just as a fish is unaware of the water it swims in, we can easily become blind to the ways of the world if we are not careful. It is crucial to constantly scrutinize our surroundings, making sure that we are not the ones being served at the table of deceit and temptation.

Vigilance in Relationships:
As you navigate through life, remember that not everyone who appears supportive has your best interests at heart. It is crucial to be cautious and scrutinize those you hold close. Your tribe, the people you surround yourself with, will have a significant impact on your journey. They can lift you up or drag you down. Be aware that not everyone is a true friend and not everyone will support you in your endeavors. Remain vigilant and carefully assess the loyalty of those around you. Trust is a precious commodity, so

choose wisely whom you share it with.

Prayer

God, open my eyes to see beyond appearances. Remove those not aligned with Your plans and bring into my life those destined to support and uplift me. Help me stay vigilant in relationships, recognizing the true intentions of those around me. Keep me woke to the enemy's schemes and guide me in wisdom and discernment. Amen.

∞ ∞ ∞

Reflection Question

Stay Woke:
How do you interpret the concept of "staying woke" in the context of your spiritual journey and daily life? Reflect on instances where being vigilant and aware has protected you from potential deception or harm. How can you cultivate a mindset of spiritual alertness in your walk with Christ?

Vigilance in Relationships:
Consider the relationships in your life, both personal and professional. Are there instances where you need to exercise more discernment in trusting others? Reflect on the impact of surrounding yourself with either supportive or unsupportive individuals. How can you strengthen your ability to discern the loyalty and intentions of those around you?

Scrutinizing Your Environment:
In what ways do you actively scrutinize your environment to avoid being misled or deceived? Reflect on the importance of being discerning in your choices, beliefs, and the information you consume. How can you incorporate spiritual discernment into your decision-making process?

Prayer for Awareness:
Take a moment to pray for God's guidance and awareness in your life. Ask for discernment in relationships, wisdom in decision-making, and protection from deception. Reflect on the role prayer plays in keeping you spiritually alert. How can you make prayer a consistent and intentional practice in staying woke and vigilant?

Day 17 – Guarding Your Mental Landscape

"Mulch your mind with God's truth"

Scripture
2 Corinthians 4:4 - "*the god of this world has blinded the minds of unbelievers, to keep them from seeing the light of the gospel of the glory of Christ.*"

Mindful Mulching:
In the world of real estate, creating an alluring curb appeal is vital to catching the eye of potential buyers. The careful arrangement and design of landscaping plays a crucial role in this process, specifically through the practice of mulching. This layer of organic matter acts as a protective barrier for delicate plant roots, shielding them from the harsh elements of nature. Just like how mulch safeguards plants, our minds also require a similar process to fend off destructive thoughts planted by external forces. It serves as a shield against the enemy's attempts to penetrate and harm our innermost thoughts and beliefs.

Deceptive Weeds of the Mind:
Like invasive weeds choking the life out of vibrant plants, negative thoughts injected by the enemy can sap your mental strength and hinder your growth. The god of this world prowls like a predator, seeking to blind minds and keep them from seeing the light of God's truth. It is crucial to be vigilant and confront these

deceptive thoughts that seek to rob you of your worth, value, and significance. Just as a gardener must constantly tend to their garden, we must tend to our minds and uproot any damaging seeds planted by the enemy. Only then can we thrive in the sunlight of God's love and grace.

The Power of God's Truth:
In his letter to the Corinthians, Paul warns against the enemy's cunning ways of manipulating and deceiving our thoughts. To combat this, we must nurture our minds with God's truth. We must recognize that we are masterpieces created by God for good works. Let go of any false beliefs that deem you unworthy or a failure. Walk boldly, fully aware of your purpose and worth.

Prayer
Father, help me see myself as You see me. Guide me through the deception planted by the enemy, freeing me from thoughts of worthlessness. Mulch my mind with Your truth, so I can walk confidently in the purpose You have prepared for me. Amen.

∞∞∞

Reflection Questions
Mindful Mulching:
In what ways do you currently engage in a "mulching process" for your mind? Reflect on practices that protect your mental well-being and shield you from negative influences. How can you enhance your mental landscape to promote a healthier mindset?

Deceptive Weeds of the Mind:
Identify any negative thoughts or beliefs that may have taken root in your mind. How do these thoughts challenge your sense of worth, value, or significance? Reflect on how the enemy might use deception to hinder your spiritual growth. What steps can you take to uproot these deceptive "weeds" from your mind?

The Power of God's Truth:

Consider the transformative power of God's truth in your life. How has embracing God's truth positively influenced your self-perception and confidence? Reflect on specific Bible verses or promises that reinforce your worth and purpose in Christ. How can you integrate these truths into your daily mindset?

Prayer for Mental Preservation:

Take a moment to pray for mental preservation and clarity. Ask God to reveal any deceptive thoughts and replace them with His truth. Reflect on the role prayer plays in maintaining a healthy mental landscape. How can you make prayer a consistent practice in guarding your mind from negative influences?

Day 18 - The Internal Battle: Cultivating the Mind

"The condition of your mind dictates the position of your future."

Scripture
Proverbs 16:9 – *"The mind of man plans his way, but the Lord directs his steps."*

The Zoo Paradox:
As children press their faces against the thick glass walls, a sense of wonder washes over them at the sight of majestic lions and playful monkeys. But as they marvel at the exotic creatures before them, an underlying paradox presents itself. These magnificent animals, once roaming free in vast savannas and dense rainforests, are now confined to carefully crafted exhibits for human entertainment. And like these animals, we too struggle with a constant battle between conforming to societal norms and embracing our own unique freedom. The zoo is a microcosm of this inner conflict, reminding us of our complex relationship with both captivity and liberty.

Human Conformity:
The creatures confined within the walls of captivity endure the same consequences as we do when we conform. Our unique beings, fashioned in the likeness of a higher power, struggle with our tarnished selves tainted by societal expectations. Giving into the lure of worldly desires confines us to a prison of emptiness, constraining the true essence of our divine purpose and potential.

Cultivating the Mind:
In order to break away from the pressure of conforming, we must tend to our minds like a garden. We uproot harmful thoughts and cultivate beliefs that align with God's wisdom. In Romans 12:2, we are encouraged to transform ourselves by renewing our minds, instead of simply conforming. This involves actively working towards aligning our thoughts with the teachings of God's Word.

Stinking Thinking:
When we allow negative thoughts to take hold, our minds become polluted with stinking thinking. To create a positive future, we must train our minds to adopt new fundamental beliefs and make decisions based on God's teachings. The state of our minds determines the direction of our future.

Prayer
Lord, reveal any thoughts contrary to Your purpose for me. Guide me through the process of cultivating wisdom in my mind, freeing me from the bondage of stinking thinking. May my thoughts align with Your Word and shape a future filled with Your purpose. Amen.

∞∞∞

Reflection Questions
The Zoo Paradox:
Reflect on the analogy of the zoo and how it relates to the internal battle of conformity and freedom. In what ways do you find yourself conforming to worldly influences, similar to animals in captivity? How has this conformity hindered your full expression of who God created you to be?

Human Conformity:
Consider the impact of conformity to worldly pleasures on your spiritual life. How has conformity affected your relationship with God and your understanding of your identity in Him? Reflect on areas where you feel trapped in a "cage of desolation" and desire freedom.
Cultivating the Mind:

Explore the concept of cultivating your mind as you would a garden. What deliberate efforts can you make to remove detrimental thoughts and nurture beliefs aligned with God's wisdom? How can you actively engage in renewing your mind, as suggested in Romans 12:2?

Stinking Thinking:
Identify any instances of "stinking thinking" in your life—thoughts that are void of God's wisdom. How have these thoughts influenced your decisions and actions? Consider the consequences of allowing such thinking to persist and its impact on shaping your future.

Prayer for Mind Cultivation:
Pray about the process of mind cultivation. Ask God to reveal and transform any thoughts that hinder your spiritual growth. Seek His guidance in aligning your thoughts with His Word and shaping a future filled with His purpose. How can prayer become a regular practice in renewing your mind?

Day 19 - Beware of Diverging Distractions

"Don't become so focused on the worm that you miss the glare of the hook."

Scripture
1 Peter 5:8 – "Be sober, be vigilant, because your adversary the devil walks about as a roaring lion, seeking whom he may devour."

The Fishing Parable:
With the gentle sound of lapping waves and the warm sun kissing their skin, fishing serves as a beloved recreational activity for many. The act of casting a line and patiently waiting for a bite offers a serene escape from daily life. But with every carefully chosen bait and concealed hook, there lies a mirror to our own temptations and vices. Like unsuspecting fish, we can easily become ensnared in the web of deceitful distractions that lure us in. Much like the struggle of a caught fish, we must fight against these destructive attractions to free ourselves and swim towards a brighter future

Deceptive Pleasures:
Like a moth drawn to the flames, we are often enticed by attractions that can put our very well-being at risk. Just as a smoker is enchanted by the immediate pleasure of nicotine, we too can be consumed by the allure of instant gratification. However, just as warnings adorn cigarette packs, Peter reminds us in 1 Peter 5:8 to resist distraction and remain vigilant against the enemy's attempts to devour us. Like a wolf waiting for its prey, the

adversary lurks in the darkness, ready to pounce on any moment of weakness. We must stay alert and stand firm in our faith to avoid falling victim to his schemes.

Satan's Deceptive Tactics:
Satan is cunning and uses deceitful tactics, disguising harmful temptations with attractive promises. He prowls around like a roaring lion, preying on our senses and distracting us from the truth. Just as Eve was lured by the beauty of the forbidden fruit in the Garden, we can be blinded by the alluring appeal of sin. Satan takes advantage of our wants and entices us away from God's righteous path.

The Glare of the Hook:
The real danger is in becoming fixated on the enticing bait, while completely disregarding the insidious hook. The devil often tempts us with our own desires, just as he did with Eve and the forbidden tree. In the same way, we can become captivated by worldly distractions and lose sight of God's truth. It is crucial that we do not allow ourselves to be blinded by the allure of the world and fall victim to the enemy's cunning schemes.

Prayer
Lord, grant me discernment to see beyond attractive distractions. Help me focus on Your truth and resist the temptations that seek to ensnare me. May my eyes be fixed on You, shielding me from the deceitful allure of the enemy. Amen.

∞∞∞

Reflection Questions
The Fishing Parable:
Reflect on the analogy of fishing as a recreational activity and how it relates

to life's distractions. Consider the serene escape that distractions may initially provide. In what ways have you experienced the allure of distractions that eventually revealed hidden hooks in your life?

Deceptive Pleasures:
Explore the concept of deceptive pleasures that jeopardize well-being. Are there specific distractions in your life that, like nicotine's allure, offer immediate pleasure but come with long-term consequences? How do these distractions hinder your spiritual growth and relationship with God?

Satan's Deceptive Tactics:
Consider the crafty tactics employed by Satan, who masquerades threats with attractive bait. How has the enemy prowled in your life, captivating your senses and leading you away from God's path? Reflect on specific instances where distractions disguised as allurements led you astray.

The Glare of the Hook:
Reflect on the danger of fixating on the bait while missing the glaring hook. In what areas of your life are you prone to becoming captivated by distractions, losing sight of God's truth? How can you remain vigilant and discern the enemy's tactics, recognizing the glare of the hook?

Prayer for Discernment:
Engage in a prayer for discernment. Ask God to grant you discernment to see beyond attractive distractions. Pray for the strength to focus on God's truth and resist temptations that seek to ensnare you. How can prayer become a regular practice in maintaining vigilance against diverging distractions?

Day 20 - A Call to Authenticity

"Originators are in, imitators are out."

Scripture
Psalm 139:13-14 – *"For you formed my inward parts; you knitted me together in my mother's womb. I praise you, for I am fearfully and wonderfully made."*

The Era of Uniqueness:
In a society where conformity reigns supreme, the concept of originality has become a distant memory. The pursuit of authenticity has been pushed aside, leaving behind an era marked by mediocrity and sameness. As we strive to imitate others instead of embracing our own uniqueness, a dark twilight has descended upon us, one where diversity is seen as an anomaly and individuality is shunned.

Created with Purpose:
God, the master craftsman, designed each of us with unparalleled uniqueness. We are fearfully and wonderfully made, a testimony to His creative genius. Our individuality, whether in skin color, eye color, or giftedness, reflects the diversity intended by the Creator (Isaiah 64:8, Genesis 1:27).

Embracing Originality:
To live authentically is to recognize the wonder of our creation. Dare to be different; it's the path to unexplored lands. But being unique comes with a price. Throughout history, individuals such as Joseph, David, Daniel, Job, Caleb, and Jesus have faced trials because of their differences but ultimately received rewards that

far outweighed the struggles.

The Cost and Rewards of Originality:
While Joseph faced slavery, his differences led him to the palace. David, deemed foolish, became King of Israel. Daniel's uniqueness brought prosperity. Job's differences led to restoration and abundance. Caleb's distinctiveness granted him a view of the Promised Land. Jesus' unique path led to a seat at the right hand of the Father.

Truth to Remember:
"Originality is in, imitators are out." God's call is not to conform but to embrace the authenticity He knit into each of us. Let us walk in the purpose for which we were created, understanding that our differences are not obstacles but invitations to experience the extraordinary plans God has for us.

Prayer
Heavenly Father, thank you for fearfully and wonderfully making me. Help me embrace the authenticity You designed within me and recognize the unique purpose for which I was created. May I walk confidently in the path You've set before me, knowing that originality is a reflection of Your creative brilliance. In Jesus' name, I pray. Amen.

∞∞∞

Reflection Questions
The Era of Uniqueness:
Reflect on the societal pressure to conform and the tendency for originality to be replaced by imitation. In what ways have you observed or experienced the challenges of embracing authenticity in a world that often values commonness?

Created with Purpose:
Consider the biblical truth that God fearfully and wonderfully made each individual. How does recognizing the diversity in creation, as intended by the

Creator, impact your perspective on uniqueness? How can you celebrate and appreciate the diversity in yourself and others?

Embracing Originality:

Explore the concept of embracing originality and daring to be different. Are there areas in your life where you feel the pressure to conform, and how does this affect your journey? Reflect on biblical figures like Joseph, David, Daniel, Job, Caleb, and Jesus, who faced challenges for their differences but reaped rewards.

The Cost and Rewards of Originality:

Consider the cost and rewards of embracing one's uniqueness, as illustrated by the experiences of biblical figures. How can you draw inspiration from their stories to navigate challenges and reap the rewards that come with authenticity?

Truth to Remember:

Reflect on the truth that "Originality is in, imitators are out." How can this truth influence your mindset and actions in various aspects of your life? How does embracing your originality align with your understanding of God's purpose for your life?

Day 21 - Reach for New Levels of Greatness

"Don't become so blinded by the things you've done that you lose sight of what's still left to be done."

Scripture
Genesis 12:1 – *"Now the Lord said to Abram, 'Go from your country and your kindred and your father's house to the land that I will show you."*

The Bucket List Journey:
In the cinematic masterpiece "The Bucket List," Jack Nicholson and Morgan Freeman bring to life two men who have been handed a devastating diagnosis: terminal cancer. This revelation sparks a flame within them, igniting a fierce desire to break free from societal norms and embrace all that life has to offer. Against all odds and despite disapproval from those around them, they embark on an adventure of unexplored possibilities, determined to make every moment count before their inevitable fate catches up with them. Their courage and fervor serve as a reminder to us all to never settle for less than what we truly want in life.

Good vs. Great:
The struggle between being good and achieving greatness is one that spans generations. It is easy to become comfortable with simply being good, but this can prevent us from reaching our full potential for excellence. To move beyond "good" and truly become great, companies must acknowledge the dangers of complacency, make necessary changes, and strive for excellence.

This mindset can also be applied to individuals who must resist settling for mediocrity and instead push themselves towards personal growth and success. The path towards greatness may be challenging and uncertain, but it is a worthwhile pursuit for those who aim to make a lasting impact.

Abraham's Journey:
Abraham's life reflects a call from God to move from the good to the great. At seventy-five, he already enjoyed a good life in Haran. Despite comfort, God called him to a new status. Abraham didn't let what he already had or societal expectations hinder his pursuit of God's greater plan.

Your Call to Greatness:
You were not made to simply go with the flow and accept mediocrity. Your true purpose is to achieve greatness. The Bible confirms your identity as a chosen people, a royal priesthood, a holy nation - called out of darkness into wonderful light (1 Peter 2:9). Believe in the power within you (1 John 4:4) and do not let complacency hold you back from the incredible opportunities that God has planned for your future.

Encouragement:
"Don't become so blinded by the things you've done that you lose sight of what's still left to be done." God's calling extends beyond your achievements; there's more to be executed and achieved. Embrace change, challenge comfort, and reach for new levels of greatness. God's plans for you transcend the boundaries of the familiar.

Prayer

Heavenly Father, thank you for calling me into greatness. Help me break free from the comfort of the familiar and pursue the new levels You have prepared for me. Remove any blinders of contentment, and may I see the opportunities You present for greatness. In Jesus' name, I pray. Amen.

∞∞∞

Reflection Questions

The Bucket List Journey:
Reflect on the concept of a "bucket list" – a list of things one wants to achieve, experience, or accomplish in their lifetime. Have you ever created a personal bucket list? If so, what are some of the items on it, and if not, what might you consider adding?

Good vs. Great:
Consider the idea that settling for "good enough" can be a hindrance to achieving greatness. Are there areas in your life where you might be content with the status quo? How can you challenge comfort and pursue positive changes to move from good to great?

Abraham's Journey:
Explore the story of Abraham and his willingness to leave the familiar and embark on a journey towards the unknown. In what ways can you relate to Abraham's journey, and are there aspects of your life where God might be calling you to step into the unknown for greater purposes?

Your Call to Greatness:
Embrace the truth that you are created for greatness. How does recognizing your identity as a chosen race, a royal priesthood, and a holy nation impact your perspective on your potential? How can you align your actions with the belief that greatness resides within you?

Encouragement:
Consider the quote, "Don't become so blinded by the things you've done that you lose sight of what's still left to be done." How can this perspective shape your outlook on your past accomplishments and motivate you to pursue new levels of greatness?

Day 22 - Overcomer of Adversity

"Don't let your potential be measured by your quit, but let it be measured by your fight."

Scripture
Philippians 3:14 – "I press on toward the goal for the prize of the upward call of God in Christ Jesus."

Olympic Runners Triumph:
In the midst of the intense competition at the 2016 Rio Olympics, a seasoned olympic runner faced a daunting challenge in the highly anticipated 10,000-meter race. In a split second, their foot tangled with another runner's and they fell to the ground, surrounded by a sea of chaos and thundering footsteps. But like a phoenix rising from the ashes, the runner defied the odds and sprung up, determined to win the gold medal. This display of unwavering determination and refusal to succumb to panic showcased the true power of resilience. Despite the momentary setback, the runner remained unshaken and focused on their ultimate potential, pushing through every obstacle with unwavering grace and strength. It was a truly inspiring feat that left a lasting impression on all who witnessed it.

Facing Life's Challenges:
When faced with obstacles, setbacks, or failures in life, it can be tempting to give into doubt and fear. Our emotions can consume us and push us towards giving up. However, we should see these moments as chances to strengthen our faith. Our true potential is not measured by how many times we quit, but by our perseverance through challenges, unwavering belief in the face of

adversity, and pursuit of God's purpose for us.

The Lion King Analogy:
In "The Lion King," we are presented with a poignant allegory that showcases the interdependence of all living things. Each species has its own role to play, just like how our individual paths come together to form a greater purpose. By accepting and embracing our differences, we can break free from self-doubt and move towards progress.

Breaking the Power of the Past:
While we can't erase past memories, we can break their power by allowing God to release us from their influence. The journey involves recognizing our worth, understanding the interconnectedness of our experiences, and pressing on toward the upward call of God.

Encouragement:
"Don't let your potential be measured by your quit, but let it be measured by your fight." Refuse to be defined by setbacks. Instead, view challenges as stepping stones toward growth and press on toward the goal set before you.

Prayer
Heavenly Father, grant me the strength to press on despite life's challenges. Help me overcome setbacks and not be defined by moments of failure. May I embrace resilience, fight through difficulties, and focus on the upward call You have for me. In Jesus' name, I pray. Amen.

∞∞∞

Reflection Questions

Facing Life's Challenges:
Consider the devotional's perspective on facing life's challenges as opportunities to build bridges of faith. How do you typically respond to challenges? Are there areas in your life where you can shift your mindset from seeing setbacks as failures to viewing them as opportunities for growth?

The Lion King Analogy:
Explore the analogy from *The Lion King* about the interconnectedness of creation and how each individual's journey contributes to a grander design. How does recognizing your unique journey and contributions free you from self-doubt and propel you forward?

Breaking the Power of the Past:
Reflect on the concept of breaking the power of the past by allowing God to release you from its influence. Are there past memories or experiences that still hold power over your present mindset? How can you seek God's help in releasing and overcoming these influences?

Encouragement:
Consider the encouragement, "Don't let your potential be measured by your quit, but let it be measured by your fight." How can you apply this perspective to your current circumstances or challenges? In what areas of your life do you need to focus on pressing on toward the goals set before you?

Day 23 - Rescued from Despair: The Divine Release

Your release is your rescue

Scripture
Psalm 34:17-18 - *"The righteous cry out, and the Lord hears them; he delivers them from all their troubles. The Lord is close to the brokenhearted and saves those who are crushed in spirit."*

Release from the Chains of Despair:
In the intricate and ever-shifting tapestry of life, there are moments when God's hand can be seen orchestrating a divine release from situations that bind us in despair. Losing a job may initially feel like a devastating setback, like being thrown into the depths of a raging river with no lifeline. But it is often in those moments that we realize this could be God's way of setting us free from a path that no longer aligns with His purpose for our lives. It's as if He is gently guiding us towards a new direction, one filled with opportunities and blessings we never could have imagined. This is what we call a divine release.

The winds of change blow fiercely, but within their gusts lies the potential for growth and transformation. Trust in the divine plan, and let go of what once held you back - for it is only then that you can soar to new heights and fulfill your true destiny.

The Weight of Despair:
When a job becomes a source of distress, it can have a negative impact on our overall well-being. In these moments of despair,

God may see fit to release us from the burden that threatens to crush our spirits. He listens to our cries and offers divine intervention to help free us.

Finding Purpose in Release:
As challenging as job loss may be, it's crucial to view it as a release rather than a setback. God's plan for your life involves seasons of change, and what seems like an ending may be the prelude to a new chapter filled with purpose and fulfillment. Release allows for renewal.

The Lord Is Close to the Brokenhearted:
In times of job loss and despair, the Lord draws near to the brokenhearted. He is not distant or indifferent to your struggles; instead, He is intimately involved in every aspect of your life. Your release from a job becomes an opportunity for God to mend and heal.

Trusting in God's Provision:
God's release from a job is an invitation to trust in His provision. While the future may seem uncertain, God is faithful to provide for His children. The release becomes a bridge to a place where you can discover new facets of God's faithfulness and experience His guidance in unexpected ways.

Prayer
Heavenly Father, I bring before You the challenges and emotions tied to the release from my job. In moments of despair, help me trust that Your plans are for my welfare. Draw near to me, O Lord, and mend the broken pieces of my heart. Guide me in the next steps, and may Your provision be evident in my life. In Jesus' name, I pray. Amen.

∞∞∞

Reflection Questions
Release from Despair:
Reflect on a time in your life when you experienced a release from a situation that initially seemed despairing. How did your perspective change over time? In what ways did God use that release for your good?

Weight of Despair:
Consider situations in your life that currently feel heavy or burdensome. How might viewing them as a potential release, orchestrated by God, change your perspective? How can trust in God's wisdom alleviate the weight of despair?

Finding Purpose in Release:
Explore the idea of viewing job loss or significant changes as a release rather than a setback. In what ways can such releases open the door to new opportunities and purposes in line with God's plan for your life?

The Lord Is Close:
Reflect on the assurance that the Lord is close to the brokenhearted. How does this knowledge impact your response to challenging situations? How can you experience God's closeness in the midst of despair?

Trusting in God's Provision:
Consider times in your life when you had to trust in God's provision during uncertain circumstances. How did God demonstrate His faithfulness? In what ways can trust in God's provision shape your response to current challenges?

Day 24 - The Blueprint of Creation: Where Mind Meets Manifestation

"Creation begins in the mind"

Scripture
Proverbs 23:7 - *"For as he thinks in his heart, so is he."*

The Genesis of Creation:
In the grand tapestry of existence, creation begins not with a simple gesture, but with the wondrous depths of imagination. Your thoughts, like masterful architects, carefully lay out the framework for the reality you are destined to inhabit. Just as God spoke the universe into being, your thoughts hold the power to shape and mold your personal universe. The vast expanse of your mind is teeming with endless possibilities and potential. With each thought, you weave a thread into the ever-expanding fabric of life, creating a unique and intricate design that is uniquely yours.

The Mind as a Canvas:
Imagine your mind as a vast, empty canvas waiting to be brought to life with the deliberate strokes of intention. Each thought that you choose to entertain acts as a pigment, adding depth and dimension to the overall masterpiece. With each brushstroke, you have the power to create your own reality and shape the course of your existence. Every contemplation and meditative moment becomes woven into the very fabric of your being, shaping who you are and who you will become. The canvas is yours to fill, so

choose your thoughts wisely for they will ultimately determine the colors that adorn the landscape of your life.

The Power of Imagination:
God, in His divine wisdom, granted you the gift of imagination—an extraordinary tool that bridges the ethereal realm of thought with the tangible world of creation. Your mind is a workshop, and imagination is the artisan crafting the designs that will eventually find expression in your reality. Imagination precedes manifestation.

Positive Thoughts, Positive Outcomes:
As the scripture wisely notes, "For as he thinks in his heart, so is he." Your thoughts mold your character, shape your actions, and ultimately determine your destiny. Positive thoughts cultivate a fertile ground for positive outcomes, whereas negative thoughts can poison the soil, hindering the growth of the beautiful possibilities planted within.

Guarding the Gates of the Mind:
Just as a city's gates are guarded to prevent unwarranted entry, so must you guard the gates of your mind. What you allow into your thoughts becomes the blueprint of your reality. Filter out negativity, doubt, and fear, and let in thoughts of faith, hope, and love. Your mental landscape determines the panorama of your life.

Prayer
Heavenly Father, I recognize the profound truth that creation begins in the mind. Help me guard my thoughts, aligning them with Your truth and purpose for my life. May the blueprint of my mind be a reflection of Your wisdom and love. Guide my imagination to conceive dreams that align with Your will. In Jesus' name, I pray. Amen.

∞∞∞

Reflection Questions

The Mind as a Canvas:
Consider your mind as a canvas awaiting the brushstrokes of intention. What thoughts and ideas have you been painting on the canvas of your mind recently? How might these thoughts influence your actions and the reality you create?

The Power of Imagination:
Reflect on the role of imagination as a bridge between thought and manifestation. How have your imaginative thoughts influenced your actions and decisions in the past? In what ways can you leverage the power of imagination for positive outcomes?

Positive Thoughts, Positive Outcomes:
Explore the connection between your thoughts and the outcomes you experience. Can you recall a situation where positive thinking led to a positive outcome? How can you intentionally cultivate positive thoughts to influence your present and future?

Guarding the Gates of the Mind:
Consider the analogy of guarding the gates of a city in relation to your mind. What mental "gatekeepers" can you establish to filter out negativity and foster positive thoughts? How might this practice impact your overall well-being?

Creation begins in the Mind:
Embrace the truth that creation begins in the mind. In what ways can you align your thoughts with God's truth and purpose for your life? How might this alignment positively shape your actions and the reality you are creating?

Day 25 - Authentic Rejoicing: Genuine Joy Amidst Life's Challenges

"Don't be artificially inseminated with cheers instead of jeers"

Scripture

Philippians 4:4 - *"Rejoice in the Lord always. I will say it again: Rejoice!"*

The Call to Authentic Rejoicing:

Life's journey is a tapestry woven with threads of joy and sorrow, victories and defeats. Each strand intricately intertwined to create a masterpiece unique to our own experiences. But in the midst of this intricate design, the apostle Paul beckons us with an emphatic call: "Rejoice in the Lord always. I will say it again: Rejoice!" (Philippians 4:4). This invitation is not a mere superficial cheer, an artificial injection of positive sentiments. It is a call to authentic rejoicing rooted in the unchanging nature of our Lord, as steady and enduring as the roots of an ancient oak tree that have stood firm through centuries of storms and seasons. So let us lift our hearts in true celebration, recognizing the beauty and purpose within each thread of our personal tapestries, for they all lead to a greater design crafted by the Master's loving hands.

Embracing a Realistic Perspective:

In a world often marred by challenges and uncertainties, Paul's exhortation to rejoice might seem paradoxical. Yet, his words unveil a profound truth: genuine joy transcends external circumstances. It emanates from a relationship with the Lord that remains unshaken by life's fluctuations. Authentic rejoicing is not oblivious to difficulties; rather, it stems from an unwavering confidence in God's sovereignty.

The Pitfalls of Artificial Insemination:
In the pursuit of happiness, there's a temptation to seek artificial insemination of cheers—superficial, temporary bursts of joy that rely on external stimuli. These momentary highs may be akin to a sugar rush, offering a fleeting sense of elation but leaving a void once the effects wear off. Authentic rejoicing, however, surpasses the ephemeral and dwells in the eternal.

Rooted in the Lord:
True joy is not contingent on a trouble-free existence. It is anchored in a deep, abiding connection with the Lord. When we rejoice in Him always, we acknowledge His faithfulness, even in adversity. Our joy becomes an outpouring of gratitude for His unchanging character, His redemptive love, and His promise to be with us through every trial.

The Source of Authentic Joy:
As believers, our joy is rooted in the reality of God's grace and the assurance of His eternal promises. It is a byproduct of our relationship with Christ, who overcame the world (John 16:33). Authentic rejoicing emerges when we fix our gaze on Him, acknowledging His lordship over our lives and finding solace in His unshakeable peace.

Prayer
Heavenly Father, Teach Me The Art Of Authentic Rejoicing. May My Joy Be Rooted In You, Transcending Circumstances And Finding Its Source In Your Unwavering Faithfulness. Help Me Discern The Difference Between Artificial Cheers And The Genuine Joy That Emanates From A Heart Anchored In Your Love. In Jesus' Name, I Pray. Amen.

∞∞∞

Reflection Questions

The Call to Authentic Rejoicing:
Reflect on the call to "Rejoice in the Lord always" (Philippians 4:4). How do you interpret Paul's invitation to rejoice, considering the various facets of life's journey? What challenges or victories have you faced recently that impact your ability to rejoice authentically?

Embracing a Realistic Perspective:
Consider the paradoxical nature of rejoicing in the midst of life's challenges. How does the concept of authentic rejoicing differ from a superficial pursuit of happiness? In what ways can you cultivate a realistic perspective on joy that acknowledges both difficulties and God's sovereignty?

The Pitfalls of Artificial Insemination:
Explore the idea of artificial insemination of cheers—temporary bursts of joy dependent on external stimuli. Have you experienced moments of artificial joy in your life? How can you discern between superficial happiness and the deep, lasting joy that comes from a relationship with the Lord?

Rooted in the Lord:
Reflect on the role of God's character, redemptive love, and promises in anchoring authentic joy. How does your understanding of God's faithfulness impact your ability to rejoice in all circumstances? How can you deepen your connection with the Lord to strengthen the roots of your joy?

The Source of Authentic Joy:
Consider the source of authentic joy as rooted in the reality of God's grace and eternal promises. How does your relationship with Christ contribute to the authenticity of your joy? In what ways can you fix your gaze on Him, especially during challenging times, to experience His unshakeable peace?

Day 26 - Breaking the Chains of Routine: Embracing the Wonder of God's Creation

"Routine is resistant to wonder"

Scripture
Psalm 19:1 - *"The heavens declare the glory of God; the skies proclaim the work of his hands."*

The Monotony of Routine:
Day in and day out, we are entranced by the monotonous rhythm of our daily lives. The mundane tasks of waking up, commuting, working, returning home, and sleeping weave together to form a tapestry of predictability. Routine offers a sense of stability, but with it comes a subtle resistance to wonder. In the midst of this routine, the extraordinary can often be hidden behind the ordinary. The mundane has a way of obscuring the magic that surrounds us, and we must make an effort to peel back its cloak and embrace the wonder that lies beneath.

Unlocking Wonder through God's Creation:
In Psalm 19:1, the psalmist declares, "The heavens declare the glory of God; the skies proclaim the work of his hands." Amidst the monotony of routine, the vast canvas of the skies beckons us to unlock the shackles of familiarity and embrace the wonder of God's creation. The heavens are a living masterpiece, a perpetual exhibition of God's glory painted across the cosmic canvas.

Resisting the Pull of Routine:
Routine can be resistant to wonder because it breeds familiarity that numbs our senses to the marvels surrounding us. The sunrise becomes a mere transition from night to day, the rustling leaves lose their melody, and the starlit sky fades into the background. To break free from this monotony, we must intentionally resist the pull of routine, opening our eyes to the extraordinary within the ordinary.

Discovering Divine Wonders:
God's creation is a treasury of wonders waiting to be discovered. The intricate details of a flower, the symphony of nature's sounds, the dance of sunlight on water – these are invitations to marvel at the Creator's handiwork. When we lift our gaze from the well-worn path of routine, we enter a realm where each moment becomes an encounter with divine wonders.

Cultivating a Heart of Wonder:
Cultivating a heart of wonder involves intentional shifts in perspective. Instead of rushing through routine tasks with a mechanical mindset, we can approach them with an awareness of God's presence. The ordinary moments become infused with sacredness as we recognize that every breath, every step, is a gift from our Creator.

Prayer

Heavenly Father, open my eyes to the wonders that surround me in Your creation. Help me break free from the chains of routine and discover the extraordinary within the ordinary. May my heart be attuned to the marvels of Your handiwork, declaring Your glory with every breath. In Jesus' name, I pray. Amen.

∞∞∞

Reflection Questions

The Monotony of Routine:
Consider your daily routine and how it contributes to the rhythm of your life. Are there aspects of routine that provide stability and comfort? How might routine, if unchecked, become a hindrance to embracing the wonder of God's creation?

Unlocking Wonder through God's Creation:
Reflect on Psalm 19:1, which declares the heavens as declaring the glory of God. In what ways does the natural world, particularly the skies, proclaim the work of God's hands to you? How can the beauty of creation serve as a source of wonder amidst daily routines?

Resisting the Pull of Routine:
Acknowledge the resistance routine can have on experiencing wonder. Are there specific moments in your routine where you've noticed a tendency to become numb to the extraordinary? How might intentional resistance to routine's pull open your eyes to divine wonders?

Discovering Divine Wonders:
Explore the idea that God's creation is a treasury of wonders waiting to be discovered. What are some elements of nature that you find particularly wondrous? How can you actively seek and discover divine wonders in the seemingly ordinary moments of life?

Cultivating a Heart of Wonder:
Consider practical ways to cultivate a heart of wonder in your daily life. How can you approach routine tasks with an awareness of God's presence? In what ways might a shift in perspective turn ordinary moments into sacred encounters with the Creator?

Day 27 - Rising Beyond Defeats: The Resilience of Christ's Victory

"Resilience is not the absence of defeats but the capacity to rise again"

Scripture
Romans 8:37 - "*No, in all these things we are more than conquerors through him who loved us.*"

The Power of Rising:
Like a winding road through treacherous terrain, life's journey is marked by both steep falls and soaring rises. Moments of defeat can seem all-consuming, leaving us feeling broken and battered. But it is in the moments of rising that true strength is revealed. It takes unwavering resilience and an unbreakable spirit to conquer these challenges. In the narrative of our lives, it's not just the falls that can be destructive, but also the rises that determine our ultimate path. Each rise brings new obstacles to overcome and new lessons to learn, shaping us into who we are meant to become."

The Greatest Defeat and Victory:
Reflecting on the greatest defeat and victory in history, we find Jesus' crucifixion and resurrection. At a surface level, the crucifixion appears to be the ultimate defeat – the Son of God hanging on a cross, bearing the weight of humanity's sin. Yet, it was precisely through this apparent defeat that the greatest victory was achieved. Jesus rose from the grave, conquering sin and death, and securing salvation for all who believe.

More Than Conquerors:
In Romans 8:37, the apostle Paul declares, "No, in all these things we are more than conquerors through him who loved us." The paradox lies in being "more than conquerors" through the very things that would seem like defeat. The falls, the challenges, and the struggles become the catalysts for rising stronger, not in our own might, but through the love and power of Christ.

Embracing Resilience:
Resilience is not simply avoiding defeat, but rather the inner strength to rise again after being knocked down. The powerful story of Christ's resurrection serves as a reminder that defeats do not have the final say. It is in the act of rising, empowered by His resurrection, that we find true victory. So when faced with setbacks, disappointments, or failures, hold on to the assurance that Christ's triumphant victory overcame the darkest of defeats and His resurrecting strength is readily available to lift you out of any circumstance you may encounter. The power of His redemption lingers in the air, urging us to keep pressing on with unwavering determination and unshakeable faith.

The Call to Rise:
Every rise after a fall is an invitation to participate in Christ's victory. It's acknowledging that defeats don't define us; rather, they become platforms for God's transformative work. As you face challenges, hear the call to rise – rise above doubt, rise above fear, and rise above circumstances. Christ's victory is your victory.

Prayer
Lord Jesus, thank You for Your triumphant resurrection that turned defeat into victory. Grant me the strength to rise above every challenge and setback. In moments of difficulty, let Your resurrection power fill me with hope and resilience. May I embrace the truth that, in You, I am more than a conqueror. In Your name, I pray. Amen.

∞∞∞

Reflection Questions

The Power of Rising:
Reflect on a time in your life when you faced a significant setback or defeat. What did it feel like in the moment, and how did you navigate through it? What lessons or strengths did you discover in the process of rising?

The Greatest Defeat and Victory:
Consider the crucifixion and resurrection of Jesus Christ. How do you perceive the apparent defeat of the crucifixion in light of the ultimate victory of the resurrection? What insights can you draw from this paradox for your own experiences of defeat and victory?

More Than Conquerors:
In Romans 8:37, Paul declares believers to be "more than conquerors." What does this phrase mean to you in the context of facing challenges and defeats? How does the love of Christ play a role in being more than a conqueror?

Embracing Resilience:
Explore the concept of resilience as the capacity to rise again. How do you define resilience in your own life? In what ways have you experienced or witnessed resilience in the face of adversity?

The Call to Rise:
Consider the call to rise as an invitation to participate in Christ's victory. How does this perspective change the way you view defeats and setbacks? In what areas of your life do you sense the call to rise, trusting in the resurrection power of Christ?

Day 28 - Past Problems, Present Praise

"The problem of your past will become the praise of your present"

Scripture

Psalm 103:2-5 - *"Praise the Lord, my soul, and forget not all his benefits—who forgives all your sins and heals all your diseases, who redeems your life from the pit and crowns you with love and compassion, who satisfies your desires with good things so that your youth is renewed like the eagle's."*

Transforming Problems into Praise:

Life is a winding path, full of twists and turns that shape us into who we are. Each one of us carries a unique set of experiences, some marked by challenges that tested our strength, mistakes that taught us valuable lessons, and hurts from the past that have made us stronger. But in the midst of it all, there is beauty in our faith and the transformative power of God's love. What was once a stumbling block on our journey can become the very foundation for our present and future praise. The scars we bear tell stories of resilience and redemption, serving as reminders of the grace and mercy that guide us along the way.

Forgiveness and Healing:

In Psalm 103:2-5, the psalmist reflects on the manifold benefits of God, including forgiveness, healing, redemption, and the overflowing love and compassion of the Lord. It's a profound reminder that God doesn't merely address one aspect of our lives but tends to the entirety of our being. Your past mistakes and sins are not beyond the reach of God's forgiveness and redemption.

Redemption from the Pit:
The powerful imagery of God reaching down to rescue your life from the depths of a pit paints a vivid picture of overcoming despair, shame, and hopelessness. Your past may have been marred by deep pits of regret and mistakes, but with God's redemptive power, you can rise above those depths and stand on firm ground once again. As if pulled up by unseen hands, you can break free from the grip of darkness and emerge into the light of hope and restoration.

Crowned with Love and Compassion:
God doesn't stop at redemption; He crowns you with love and compassion. The very areas of brokenness become adorned with God's transformative love. Your past struggles become a platform for the display of God's grace and compassion in your life.

Satisfaction and Renewal:
The psalmist further highlights that God satisfies your desires with good things. Your past problems don't define your present; rather, God satisfies your heart with His goodness. As you surrender your past to Him, He renews your strength, much like the eagle's youth is renewed.

From Problem to Praise:
What was once a problem in your past – be it sin, brokenness, or mistakes – becomes an opportunity for praise when surrendered to God. His forgiveness, healing, redemption, and transformative love turn the narrative of your life. Your testimony becomes a testament to God's power to bring beauty out of ashes.

Prayer
Heavenly Father, thank You for Your transformative love that turns my past problems into present praise. I surrender my mistakes, sins, and struggles to You. Redeem and crown my life with Your love and

compassion. May my story be a testimony to Your power to bring beauty out of ashes. In Jesus' name, I pray. Amen.

∞∞∞

Reflection Questions
Transforming Problems into Praise:
Reflect on a specific problem or mistake from your past that you have struggled to let go. How does the idea of transforming past problems into present praise resonate with you? What would it look like to surrender that situation to God and allow Him to work?

Forgiveness and Healing:
Consider the promise of forgiveness and healing in Psalm 103:2-5. How does the assurance of God's forgiveness impact your perspective on past mistakes? In what ways have you experienced God's healing in your life?

Redemption from the Pit:
The psalmist speaks of God redeeming our lives from the pit. Can you identify areas in your past where you felt trapped in a "pit" of despair, shame, or hopelessness? How has God's redemptive power lifted you from those depths?

Crowned with Love and Compassion:
Reflect on the imagery of being crowned with love and compassion. In what ways have you experienced God's love and compassion in the midst of past struggles? How does God's love transform the way you view your own brokenness?

Satisfaction and Renewal:
Psalm 103:5 speaks of God satisfying your desires with good things and renewing your strength. How have you seen God satisfy your heart with His goodness? In what areas of your life do you need His renewal and strength?

From Problem to Praise:
Consider the invitation to turn your past problems into present praise. How might your testimony become a testament to God's power to bring beauty out of ashes? In what ways can you actively surrender your past to God and embrace the praise He has in store for your present?

Day 29 - Embracing the Giver to Receive the Gift

"You can't get what God's got for you if you don't got the God that has it"

Scripture
James 4:8 - *"Draw near to God, and he will draw near to you."*

Accessing God's Promises:
In our journey through life, we often eagerly await the fulfillment of God's blessings, breakthroughs, and promises. Yet, it is vital to understand that our ability to receive these gifts from Him is intricately connected to our relationship with Him. As James 4:8 reminds us, when we draw near to God with open hearts and minds, He draws nearer to us in return. This powerful principle speaks to the importance of developing an intimate connection with the ultimate Giver - for it is this closeness that sets us up to receive the abundance of His blessings and plans for our lives.

God's Abundant Blessings:
God, as the ultimate Giver, desires to pour out blessings, favor, and purpose into our lives. However, He longs for more than transactional interactions. God desires a relationship, an intimate connection where we draw near to Him not just for what He can give but for who He is.

The Significance of Relationship:
Imagine a child who eagerly awaits a gift from their parent. The joy isn't merely in the gift itself but in the relationship with

the one giving it. In the same way, God wants us to approach Him, not just seeking His blessings, but desiring to know Him intimately. The closeness of our relationship with God magnifies the significance of the gifts He bestows.

Getting What God's Got:
The phrase "You can't get what God's got for you if you don't got the God that has it" encapsulates a profound truth. God's blessings and promises are intricately linked to His character, nature, and the depth of our connection with Him. It's not about our efforts to attain, but about our surrender and closeness to the One who gives generously.

Drawing Near with Faith:
To draw near to God is an act of faith and surrender. It involves seeking Him in prayer, engaging with His Word, and cultivating a heart of worship. As we draw near, God responds by drawing near to us, unveiling the depths of His love, wisdom, and the blessings He has prepared.

Prayer
Heavenly Father, I desire to draw near to You, not just for the blessings You provide but for the beauty of knowing You intimately. Help me cultivate a deep and meaningful relationship with You. I surrender my desires, dreams, and needs to You, trusting that as I draw near to You, You will draw near to me. In Jesus' name, I pray. Amen

∞∞∞

Reflection Questions
Awakening!
What does it mean to you to "awake" from a state of unawareness or slumber in your life? Reflect on a time when you felt a sense of enlightenment or clarity about your identity and purpose.

Persevere and Attain

How do you interpret the saying, "Good things come to those who chase after them" in your own life? What goals or dreams are you currently pursuing, and how can you actively work toward attaining them?

Open Your Eyes
In what areas of your life do you need to be more aware and vigilant? How can you discern between genuine support and potential undermining in your relationships?

Mental Preservation
How do you currently practice "mulching" your mind with positive influences and God's word? In what ways can negative thoughts and influences be harmful to your personal growth and potential?

The Internal Battle
Reflect on instances where your corrupted-self influenced your thoughts or actions negatively. How did you overcome or learn from those situations? What steps can you take to renew your mind and align your thoughts with God's wisdom?

Beware of Diverging Distractions
How do you recognize and resist distractions that can lead you away from your goals or values? In what areas of your life might you be enticed by deceptive "baits" that can hinder your progress?

A Call to Authenticity
In what ways do you embrace your uniqueness and resist the pressure to conform? How can your distinctiveness contribute positively to your community and relationships?

Reach for New Levels of Greatness
Are you currently settling for "good enough" in any aspect of your life? What steps can you take to transition from a mindset of "good" to one of "great"?

Overcomer of Adversity
Reflect on a time when you faced a significant setback. How did you overcome it, and what did you learn from the experience? How can moments of adversity be opportunities for growth and resilience?

The Problem of Your Past
Consider challenges or mistakes from your past. How have they shaped your present, and what positive aspects have emerged from those experiences? In what ways can you turn past problems into praise for your present?

Day 30 - The Power of Resilient Growth

"Don't let your circumstances silence you, let them grow you"

Scripture

Romans 5:3-4 – *"Not only that, but we rejoice in our sufferings, knowing that suffering produces endurance, and endurance produces character, and character produces hope."*

Embracing Growth in Adversity:

Like a carousel, life is filled with both joyous and challenging seasons. While we all relish in the highs of triumph and success, it is often in the midst of difficulties that our character is truly tested and fortified. In Romans 5:3-4, we are reminded that even in the face of suffering, there is a profound purpose - a purpose that molds us into more resilient individuals and leads us towards enduring strength, admirable character, and ultimately, unwavering hope. As each hurdle is overcome, it's as if another layer of armor is added to our souls, preparing us for whatever may come next on this unpredictable journey called life.

Triumph through Challenges:

When faced with adversity, we have a choice: let it defeat us or use it to become stronger. Like a seed pushing through the ground towards the sun, our ability to persevere through tough times can result in significant personal growth. Rather than letting challenging circumstances silence us, we can allow them to shape us into more resilient individuals.

Suffering Produces Endurance:
The process begins with endurance. When faced with trials, enduring the hardships builds a tenacity within us. It's the ability to press on, to withstand the storms, and to remain steadfast in our faith. Endurance is a muscle that strengthens through resistance.

Endurance Produces Character:
As we endure, character is refined. The challenges we face expose aspects of our character that need refinement. It's through the struggles that we learn perseverance, patience, and humility. Our character is shaped and molded as we navigate through the difficulties with faith and trust in God.

Character Produces Hope:
The culmination of enduring and developing character is the birth of hope. Hope is not wishful thinking; it's a confident expectation in the goodness and faithfulness of God. The hope that emerges from trials is a resilient hope – a hope that transcends circumstances because it is anchored in the unchanging nature of God.

Growing Through Every Season:
Just as plants grow through both sunshine and rain, our lives have seasons of joy and seasons of adversity. Embracing growth in challenging times positions us for a future filled with hope. Every trial becomes a stepping stone, every difficulty becomes a classroom, and every setback becomes a setup for a comeback.

Prayer

Heavenly Father, thank you for the assurance that even in the midst of challenges, You are working in me. Help me to embrace the growth that comes through adversity. May I find endurance, see character refined, and experience a resilient hope that is firmly anchored in Your goodness. In Jesus' name, I pray. Amen.

∞∞∞

Reflection Questions

Endurance: Reflect on a challenging time in your life. How did you navigate through it? What did you learn about yourself and your ability to endure hardships?

Character: Consider the trials that have shaped your character. In what ways have difficulties refined aspects of your character, such as perseverance, patience, or humility?

Hope: Think about a specific situation where hope emerged from a challenging circumstance. How did your perspective change, and how did your confidence in God's faithfulness grow?

Resilience: Identify areas in your life where you desire to cultivate resilience. What steps can you take to build endurance, refine character, and foster a resilient hope in these areas?

God's Faithfulness: Recall moments from your past when God proved faithful during challenging times. How can reflecting on God's faithfulness in the past strengthen your hope for the future?

Encouragement: Consider someone you know who is currently facing adversity. How can you encourage them to embrace growth in their challenges and find hope in the midst of difficulties?

Prayer: Spend time in prayer, surrendering your challenges to God. Ask for His guidance in enduring, refining your character, and finding a resilient hope in Him.

Epilogue

As we close the pages of "Sacred Seasons: A Daily Devotional for Life's Transformations," we reflect on the profound journey we've traversed together. Through the changing seasons of life, we've explored the depths of scriptural wisdom, finding solace, inspiration, and guidance for every step of our pilgrimage.

Just as the seasons of nature continue in their perpetual dance, so too does the rhythm of our lives echo the timeless truths embedded in sacred texts. In these pages, we've witnessed the blooming of hope in the spring, basked in the warmth of faith during the summer, embraced the transformative hues of autumn's lessons, and found solace in the quietude of winter's reflection.

Our journey together has been a reminder that life's transformations are sacred; they are opportunities for growth, resilience, and deeper communion with the divine. Whether you find yourself in the midst of a vibrant spring or navigating the serene stillness of winter, know that each season brings its unique blessings and challenges.

As we part ways, let the lessons learned within these daily reflections linger in your heart. May you carry the wisdom, love, and grace discovered in these pages into the unfolding seasons of your life. Remember that, just as nature springs to life after winter's rest, so too can your spirit experience renewal and rebirth.

May your journey be graced with unwavering faith, enduring hope, and boundless love. Whatever the season, may you find the divine presence guiding and sustaining you. As you continue to navigate life's sacred seasons, may your heart be filled with gratitude for the beauty of the journey.

Blessings and peace,
Dr. Jovan T. Davis

Acknowledgement

I extend heartfelt gratitude to God, the source of all wisdom and inspiration, for guiding the creation of "Sacred Seasons: A Daily Devotional for Life's Transformations." This journey has been a testament to His grace, mercy, and unwavering presence.

I express deep appreciation to Empowerment Center International, Inc. for being the nurturing soil where seeds of faith have grown and flourished. The spiritual foundation cultivated within these walls has profoundly influenced this devotional, and I am grateful for the loving community that embodies the principles of God's Word.

To my children, your joy, curiosity, and love have been a constant source of inspiration. Your presence has illuminated the path of this project, reminding me of the simplicity and purity of faith through the eyes of children.

To my mother, your unwavering support, encouragement, and prayers have been the bedrock of strength throughout this endeavor. Your love is a reflection of God's love, and I am profoundly blessed to share this journey with you.

This devotional is a collective effort, and I am thankful for the contributions of everyone who has been a part of it. May the words within these pages bring inspiration, encouragement, and a deep sense of connection with God's transformative love.

Made in the USA
Columbia, SC
22 March 2025

8c1af033-54e9-45dd-a1cd-72812572b1cfR01